Academic Writing Skills

Teacher's Manual 3

Zachary Blalock   Peter Chin

Samuel Reid   Sean Wray   Yoko Yamazaki

Shaftesbury Road, Cambridge CB2 8EA, United Kingdom

One Liberty Plaza, 20th Floor, New York, NY 10006, USA

477 Williamstown Road, Port Melbourne, VIC 3207, Australia

314–321, 3rd Floor, Plot 3, Splendor Forum, Jasola District Centre, New Delhi – 110025, India

103 Penang Road, #05–06/07, Visioncrest Commercial, Singapore 238467

Cambridge University Press & Assessment is a department of the University of Cambridge.

We share the University's mission to contribute to society through the pursuit of education, learning and research at the highest international levels of excellence.

www.cambridge.org

First published 2013

20 19 18 17 16 15 14 13 12 11 10 9

Printed in Great Britain by CPI Group (UK) Ltd, Croydon CR0 4YY

ISBN 978-1-107-63152-6 paperback Teacher's Manual 3
ISBN 978-1-107-61193-1 paperback Student's Book 3

Cambridge University Press & Assessment has no responsibility for the persistence or accuracy of URLs for external or third-party internet websites referred to in this publication and does not guarantee that any content on such websites is, or will remain, accurate or appropriate.

Contributors: Zachary Blalock, Peter Chin, Samuel Reid, Sean Wray, Yoko Yamazaki
Editor: Sean Wray

Academic Writing Skills has been developed by the Research and Development team at Waseda University International Co., Ltd., Tokyo.

Contents

Introduction to the Teacher's Manual

Academic Writing Skills is a three-level series which introduces the essential skills and strategies required to compose academic essays. *Academic Writing Skills 3* is the third book in the series. It contains four units, with each divided into parts (15 parts total in the book). There are also three appendices at the end of the book.

The *Academic Writing Skills 3 Teacher's Manual* has two parts:

Part 1: Lesson plans for each part of each unit

Part 2: The answer key to the exercises

General tips on using the textbook in class

For teachers and students, the textbook is designed to be followed directly. Therefore, each part of each unit has the following features:

1. **Sections introducing teaching points** which describe a particular aspect of academic writing.

2. **Examples and exercises** to help deepen students' understanding of the teaching points.

To best utilize the book's features and class time, it is suggested that teachers:

1. **Avoid lengthy explanations**
   - Elicit key words and concepts from the students whenever possible.
   - Use concept check questions to make sure students understand both the components of an essay and their purpose.

2. **Assign homework**
   - **Reading**   Reading of particular teaching points from the textbook can be assigned as homework. This will help when teaching these points in class, as students will be better able to answer questions on the points.
   - **Writing**   The textbook presents individual aspects of essay writing, but does not contain a specific essay writing task. It is recommended that an essay writing task be assigned to supplement the lessons. Students can apply what they learn in each lesson to this writing task so that by a certain point in the course, they will have a completed academic essay.

Lesson plans

How to use the lesson plans

The lesson plans in this teacher's manual supplement the textbook by offering suggestions for:

- presenting the teaching points (the explanation under each section heading).
- conducting the practice exercises.

There are a number of suggestions for each section. These suggestions are not meant to be followed in order. Rather, they should be viewed as a menu to choose from. Teachers should feel free to use some, all, or none of these ideas, or alternatively to supplement the textbook with their own ideas.

Text in the lesson plans that appears in italics denotes a suggested question or useful information to ask or share with students. Answers to the suggested questions appear in bold and follow (Answer) or (Possible answer).

Difficult concepts and skills

The *Academic Writing Skills* textbook series presents writing concepts and skills simply and concisely, and students should certainly read these explanations. However, some of the points may be difficult for students to grasp initially just by reading the textbook. Therefore, prepare students for difficult points by doing an introductory activity. Many of the first options in the lesson procedures are designed to generate thinking on a concept or skill before students open their textbook. Doing these activities should make the textbook's explanation easier for students to understand.

Many of the lesson procedures also have points to "emphasize" – which should help students further understand and remember the most critical points of each section. Basically, try to explain points concisely. Again, lengthy explanations are likely to confuse rather than help students. The aim during every lesson should be to try to get students to the "exercise" stage of a section.

Doing the exercises

All of the exercises have multiple options as to how they can be done. The options state whether students are to initially work individually, or collaboratively in pairs or small groups. The option chosen should depend on the students' level, both in English and the ability to comprehend the target concept or skill. For example:

- Higher-level students – consider having students do an exercise individually at the start, and then collaborate with others later in the exercise.
- Lower-level students or for particularly difficult concepts or skills – consider having students do an exercise collaboratively from the beginning.

Before the teacher checks answers with the whole class, the answer check may also be done collaboratively by students initially, which gives them an opportunity to spot mistakes and decide appropriate corrections – an effective way to reinforce their knowledge of the concepts and skills. At the end of an exercise, though, teachers should always elicit and confirm answers to check students' understanding.

Also, many of the exercises have multiple items. Reminders are given at the beginning of these exercises suggesting that students do no more than one, two, or even three items at a time before doing an answer check. Often, doing all of an exercise's items in a row without an answer check may be difficult for students and may make them lose focus.

Note too that some exercises ask students to choose the best/most suitable answer. In these cases, students should also discuss the problems with the less suitable answers.

Making classes active

Perhaps more than in other types of English skills classes, there is a great risk of students losing their motivation. Whereas English conversation or presentation skills classes often have students talking actively, a writing class can be tedious if all students do is read and write throughout a lesson. This is why many of the options suggested in the lesson procedures are comprised of collaborative work in pairs or small groups. This keeps students active and reinforces learning as students have the chance to exchange ideas with their peers.

A class could also become more active by:
- Having students switch pairs or small groups several times during class.
- Enlarging copies of a particular exercise and having students:
  1. work collaboratively to complete the exercise on one of the enlarged copies.
  2. post their work (using tape) on one of the classroom walls.
  3. walk around in pairs or small groups looking at the other students' posted answers.

Basically, look for opportunities to get students up and moving to make the class more active.

Review of lessons

Learning will be reinforced by reviewing previously taught points. To review:
- Spend time at the beginning of class having students discuss in pairs or small groups what they had learned in the previous class.
- Spend time at the end of class having students discuss what they had learned in that class.
- Save a few of the items in particular exercises and have students do them in a later class.

UNIT 1

Part 1
Understanding the essay prompt

Section 1 | ## Identifying the requirements

Option 1

1. Introduce the idea of interpreting the essay prompt by asking the following:
   - *What was a question prompt you recently had to write an essay for?*
2. Have students work in pairs or small groups to discuss the question.
3. Elicit answers.
4. Then write the following on the board:
   - *After reading an essay prompt, what are some things you should do before writing?*
5. Have students work in pairs or small groups to discuss the question.
6. Elicit answers and write them on the board.

Option 2

1. Have students read the explanations in the textbook on page 2 under "Identifying the requirements," but stop before they get to "Requirements for the essay."
2. As students are reading, write the following question on the board:
   - *What are the two main parts of an essay prompt?*
3. Then, with books closed, have students in pairs or small groups answer the question.
4. Elicit answers and write them on the board.
5. Check answers. (Answers: **1. the general topic, 2. requirements for the essay**)

   Emphasize:
   - *The first step after reading an essay prompt is to make sure you understand what the essay prompt is asking you to do.*
   - *Even if an essay is well written, if it does not directly answer the essay prompt, then it may be given a low grade for not completing the assigned task.*

Requirements for the essay
Option 1

1. Write the following on the board:
   - *Compare the health care systems of France and the United States.*

   Leave some space, then write:
   - *What type of essay do you need to write based on this prompt? What key word tells you this?*
2. Have students look at Appendix A, page 130, and in pairs or small groups discuss the question on the board.

3. Elicit answers. (Answers: **A compare and contrast essay; from the key word "compare"**)
4. Then ask: *Should you include your own opinion in the essay?*
5. Elicit answers. (Answer: **No, comparisons made in an academic essay should only be based on facts or information gathered from research. It should be up to the reader to decide which may be better.**)
6. Then in the space under the essay prompt on the board, add the following:
   - *Then evaluate the more successful of the two in terms of overall public health.*

   (So the full prompt on the board should eventually be:
   Compare the health care systems of France and the United States. Then evaluate the more successful of the two in terms of overall public health.)
7. Then ask: *Should you include your own opinion in the essay?*
8. Elicit and confirm answers. (Answer: **Yes, as indicated by the word "evaluate" in the second part of the prompt.**)

Option 2

1. Have students read the explanations in the textbook.
2. As students are reading, write the following on the board:
   - *What are four requirements in many essay prompts?*
   - *What are some instructional words which indicate:*
     - *Recall?*
     - *Analysis?*
     - *Synthesis?*
     - *Evaluation?*
   - *When should an objective opinion be provided?*
3. Have students work in pairs or small groups to discuss the questions.
4. Elicit answers and write them on the board.
5. Confirm answers.
   (Answers)
   - **Four requirements – recall, analysis, synthesis, evaluation**
   - **Instructional words – See table on textbook page 3.**
   - **Objective opinion – when the essay prompt asks for an evaluation**

   Emphasize:
   - *Look for certain instructional words in the prompt to know what is required of the essay.*

Exercise 1

1. Have students work individually to complete the exercise.
2. When done, have students compare answers with a partner.
3. Elicit answers.

Section 2 | Understanding longer essay prompts

Option 1

1. Have students read the long essay prompt on page 4.
2. As students are reading, write the following on the board:
   - *What is the main requirement in this prompt?*
3. Have students work in pairs or small groups to discuss the question.
4. Confirm answer. (Answer: **Assess how much countries should rely on nuclear energy to help meet this goal** [curbing reliance on fossil fuels] **and their energy needs.**)
5. Then write the following on the board:
   - *What should you do if you do not completely understand a long essay prompt?*
6. Have students work in pairs or small groups to discuss the question.
7. Elicit answers and write them on the board.
8. Confirm answer.
   (Answer)
   - **Create an outline of the essay prompt – Find the topic of the essay prompt, then distinguish the main requirement from sub-requirements. [Refer students to the outline structure on page 5.]**
   - **If there are still questions about the prompt, ask the professor directly.**

Option 2

1. Have students read the explanations in the textbook on pages 4–5 (both under the Section 2 heading and under "Identifying requirements in longer essay prompts").
2. As students are reading, write the following on the board:
   - *Why are long essay prompts often challenging?*
   - *How can the requirements in a long essay prompt be identified and organized?*
3. Have students work in pairs or small groups to discuss the questions.

4. Elicit answers and write them on the board.
5. Confirm answers.
   (Answers)
   - **Long essay prompts – difficult to identify topic; there are multiple requirements**
   - **How to identify and organize – Circle the instructional words indicating a requirement, then create an outline distinguishing the main requirement from sub-requirements.**

Exercise 2

Do the items one or two at a time and follow any option below. Doing all four items in a row without an answer check may be difficult for students.

Option 1

1. Have students work individually to complete the exercise.
2. When done, have students compare answers with a partner.
3. Elicit answers.

Option 2

1. Divide the class into pairs or small groups.
2. Have students work collaboratively to complete the exercise.
3. Elicit answers.

Option 3

1. Follow steps one and two of Option 2 above.
2. Re-divide students into new pairs or groups so they are sitting with at least one new person.
3. Have them compare answers with each other.
4. Elicit answers.

Option 4

1. Go through the exercise one prompt at a time.
2. For each prompt, write the outline skeleton on the board (see the layout of the outline skeleton for each prompt below).
3. Have students individually or in pairs complete the exercise in their book using the outline skeleton on the board as a guide.
4. Have students compare answers with another student or pair.
5. Elicit answers and fill in the skeleton on the board.

6. Confirm answers. (Answers: **See answer key in this book on page 56**.)

(For essay prompt 1)

Main requirement:
  – **Sub-requirement 1:**
  – **Sub-requirement 2:**
    – **Sub-sub-requirement:**

(For essay prompt 2)

Main requirement:
  – **Sub-requirement 1:**
  – **Sub-requirement 2:**

(For essay prompt 3)

Main requirement:
  – **Sub-requirement 1:**
    – **Sub-sub-requirement:**

(For essay prompt 4)

Main requirement:
  – **Sub-requirement 1:**
    – **Sub-sub-requirement:**
  – **Sub-requirement 2:**

UNIT 1

Part 2
Taking a position

Option 1

1. Write the following on the board:
   - *Do you agree or disagree with the following statement: "Globalization has had a positive influence on Asia"?*
   - *How many possible positions can a writer take in response to this essay prompt?*
2. Have students work in pairs or small groups to discuss the second question.
3. Elicit answers and write them on the board.
4. Have students look at all of the possible positions on page 7.

Option 2

1. Write the following on the board:
   - *When did the process of globalization start?*
   - *Is there a right or wrong answer to this question?*
2. Have students work in pairs or small groups to discuss the second question.
3. Elicit answers and write them on the board.
4. Confirm answers.
   (Answers)
   - **There is no absolute right or wrong answer to this question.**
   - **The position the writer takes depends on the focus of the essay with regard to globalization. For example:**
     - **If the writer focuses on communication technology's role in globalization, then it could be argued globalization began with the growth of the internet.**
     - **If the writer focuses on globalization in terms of the exploration and colonization of foreign lands, then it could be argued that globalization's origins are ancient.**
5. Then have students work in pairs or small groups to make a list of possible positions in response to the essay prompt.
6. Elicit answers and write them on the board.
7. Have students look at the possible positions on page 8.

Option 3

1. Have students read the explanations in the textbook on pages 7–8.
2. As students are reading, write the following on the board:
   - *What are the two rules for taking a position?*
3. Have students work in pairs or small groups to discuss the question.
4. Elicit answers and write them on the board.
5. Confirm answer. (Answer: **It should respond directly to the essay prompt, and it can be supported well with research.**)
   Emphasize:
   - *Taking a position does not have to mean absolute agreement or disagreement with an idea. In academic writing, the level of agreement or disagreement can vary.*

Exercise 1

Do the items one or two at a time and follow any option below. Doing all six items in a row without an answer check may be difficult for students.

Option 1

1. Have students work individually to complete the exercise.
2. When done, have students compare answers with a partner.
3. Elicit answers.

Option 2

1. Divide the class into pairs or small groups.
2. Have students work collaboratively to complete the exercise.
3. Elicit answers.

Option 3

1. Follow steps one and two of Option 2 above.
2. Re-divide students into new pairs or groups so they are sitting with at least one new person.
3. Have them compare answers with each other.
4. Elicit answers.
   Emphasize:
   - *A position can be changed later if research seems to support a different position.*

UNIT 1

Part 3
Doing research

Section 1 **Starting research**

1. When to start research

Option 1

To introduce the idea:

1. Write the following on the board:
   - *What steps should you follow when preparing to write an essay?*
     Step 1
     Step 2
     Step 3
     Step 4

2. Confirm answers.
   (Answers)
   Step 1 – Read the essay prompt
   Step 2 – Do research
   Step 3 – Finalize your position
   Step 4 – Create an outline

3. Then write the following on the board:
   - *What is the risk of taking a position before doing research?*

4. Have students work in pairs or small groups to discuss the question.

5. Elicit answers and write them on the board.

6. Confirm answers.
   (Example answers)
   Risks of taking a position before doing research:
   - **biased research of information which only supports the position**
   - **writing much of the essay then realizing the position is not supported strongly enough by research**
   - **interpretation of researched information could be skewed in favor of the position taken**

2. Asking questions

Option 1

To introduce the idea:

1. Write the following on the board:
   - *Analyze the growth of Apple's market share since the introduction of the iMac.*
   - *What information should be researched to prepare for writing this essay?*

2. Have students work in pairs or small groups to discuss the second question.

3. Elicit answers and write them on the board.

4. Have students look at the questions on page 11.

Option 2 (for both "1. When to start research" and "2. Asking questions")

1. Have students read the explanations in the textbook on pages 10 and 11.

2. As students are reading, write the following on the board:
   - *Why is it a good idea to start research before taking a position?*
   - *When starting research, what should the writer do?*

3. Have students work in pairs or small groups to discuss the questions.

4. Elicit answers and write them on the board.

5. Confirm answers.
   (Answers)
   - **Research before taking a position – It might reduce the chance of bias and save time – i.e., to avoid having to do a major rewrite because of a position change.**
   - **When starting research – Create a list of questions based on the essay prompt.**

   Emphasize:
   - *Since academic topics are often complex, consider doing research before taking a position. It might reduce the chance of bias and save time (i.e., to avoid having to do a major rewrite because of a position change).*
   - *Writers waste a lot of time doing research because they do not have specific information they are looking for. They also tend to get distracted by unrelated websites. Creating a list of questions to research keeps the writer focused and less likely to be distracted.*

Exercise 1

Do the items one or two at a time and follow any option below. Doing all six items in a row without an answer check may be difficult for students.

Option 1

1. Have students work individually to complete the exercise.

2. When done, have students compare answers with a partner.

3. Elicit answers.

Option 2

1. Divide the class into pairs or small groups.

2. Have students work collaboratively to complete the exercise.

3. Elicit answers.

Part 3 Doing research   11

Option 3

1. Follow steps one and two of Option 2 above.
2. Re-divide students into new pairs or groups so they are sitting with at least one new person.
3. Have them compare answers with each other.
4. Elicit answers.

Section 2   Keeping a research list

Option 1

1. Write the following on the board:
   - *What is the problem with gathering a lot of information through research?*
   - *How can this problem be solved?*
2. Have students work in pairs or small groups to discuss possible solutions.
3. Elicit answers and write them on the board.

Option 2

1. Have students read the explanation in the textbook on page 13 and quickly look at the sample research list that follows.
2. As students are reading, write the following on the board:
   - *What is useful about this research list?*
   - *How could this research list be improved?*
3. Have students work in pairs or small groups to discuss the questions.
4. Elicit answers and write them on the board.
5. Confirm answers.
   (Answers)
   Useful:
   - **The list is in bullet form with only relevant words, making it easier to read.**
   - **The source is placed right next to the information, making citation easier if the information is used in the essay.**

   To improve:
   - **Categorize the information according to the position supported.**

   Emphasize:
   - *Unorganized lists of information will overwhelm and confuse the writer, as it may be difficult to remember where certain information came from, and it may be more difficult to detect what position the research tends to support. An organized research list will help save the writer time and help the writer more clearly see what position the research seems to support.*

Section 3   Synthesizing research

The idea of synthesizing information and making a statement based on this synthesis may need to be introduced with simpler examples than what is presented in the book.

Option 1

1. Write the following on the board:
   - *According to the International Tourism Council, the three most popular cities in the world to visit by international tourists are 3) New York, 2) London, and 1) Paris.*
2. Under the statement, draw the following table on the board.

New York	London	Paris

3. Divide the class into groups of three or four. Assign each group one of the cities (more than one group may have the same city) and have them discuss:
   - *What aspects of your assigned city are attractive to international tourists?*
4. Elicit answers and write them on the board under the appropriate column.
   (Possible answers)
   - ***New York***
     The Empire State Building
     The Statue of Liberty
     Multi-ethnic population
     Variety of restaurants
     Central Park
     5th Ave. shopping
     Metropolitan Museum of Art
     Jazz music
     Brooklyn Bridge
     Musicals
     Museum of Modern Art
     Harlem

- *London*
  Big Ben
  Long history
  Buckingham Palace
  British Museum
  Double-decker buses
  Musicals
  Pubs
  Tate Modern Art Gallery
  Tower Bridge
  The River Thames
  Soccer
  Jack the Ripper
  The royal family
- *Paris*
  Eiffel Tower
  Champs-Elysees
  Louvre Museum
  French food
  Notre Dame
  The River Seine
  Versaille
  Fashion
  Cafés
  Arc de Triomphe

5. Then have students in pairs or small groups discuss:
   - *Based on the success of these three cities, what could a city eager for more tourists do to attract more people to visit?*

6. Elicit answers and write them on the board.

7. Confirm answers.
   (Possible answers)
   - **All three cities have famous landmark structures – New York: Empire State Building, Statue of Liberty; London: Big Ben, Buckingham Palace; Paris: Eiffel Tower, Arc de Triomphe – so perhaps a city eager for tourists should build a structure that would be attractive for them to visit.**
   - **The three cities have famous museums, so building or publicizing a museum might be a way to attract international tourists. (NOTE: The city Bilbao in Spain boosted its tourist numbers by millions after the construction of the Guggenheim Museum there.)**

Option 2

1. Divide the class into groups of three or four.

2. Have students in each group take out an item all of them are likely to have – e.g., a cell phone or even the bag they use to carry their books.

3. Then have students discuss:
   - *What do you like about your cell phone (or bag, etc.)?*

4. Elicit answers from several groups and write them on the board.

5. Then have students in pairs or small groups discuss:
   - *If you were designing a similar product, what features would you add to it to make it popular?*
   - *Popular features of cell phones are . . .*

6. Elicit answers and write them on the board.

Option 3

1. Follow Option 2 above, but for step six, instead of eliciting answers, have students mock up a design of their product.

2. Then have a representative from each group show their design and explain its features.

Option 4

1. Have students read the explanation and examples in the textbook.

2. Then, with books closed, have students in pairs or small groups summarize what they read.

3. Elicit:
   - *What are two factors that have led to the growth of Apple's market share?* (Answer: **design, manufacturing and distribution**)
   - *What evidence supports these statements?* (Answer: **the bullet points on page 14**)

   Emphasize:
   Doing research helps a writer to decide his or her position.

Exercise 2

Before starting the exercise, emphasize:
The synthesis statement is what the research shows about the essay topic.

Option 1

1. Divide the class into pairs or small groups.

2. Have students work collaboratively to complete the exercise.

3. Elicit answers.

Option 2

1. Follow steps one and two of Option 2 above.

2. Re-divide students into new pairs or groups so they are sitting with at least one new person.

3. Have them compare answers with each other.

4. Elicit answers.

Before starting the exercise, emphasize:

There is no correct answer to this question.

Option 1

1. Have students work individually to complete the exercise.

2. When done, have students compare answers with a partner.

3. Elicit answers.

Option 2

1. Divide the class into pairs or small groups.

2. Have students work collaboratively to complete the exercise.

3. Elicit answers.

Option 3

1. Follow steps one and two of Option 2 above.

2. Re-divide students into new pairs or groups so they are sitting with at least one new person.

3. Have them compare answers with each other.

4. Elicit answers.

UNIT 1

Part 4
Planning the essay

Section 1 Writing a thesis

Option 1

1. Find out what students already know about the thesis by asking:
   - *What is the thesis of an essay?*
   - *Why is the thesis the most important part of an essay?*
2. Elicit answers and write them on the board.
3. Confirm answers.
   (Answers)
   - **The thesis is a sentence which states the topic of the essay and the writer's position.**
   - **It is important because it tells the reader the purpose of the essay.**

Option 2

1. Have students read the explanation and examples in the textbook on pages 17–18, but stop before they get to "Directly responding to the essay prompt."
2. As students are reading, write the following on the board:
   - *Why is the thesis the most important part of an essay?*
   - *What does an effective thesis include?*
3. Elicit answers and write them on the board.
4. Confirm answers.
   (Answers)
   - **The thesis tells readers the purpose of the essay.**
   - **An effective thesis should clearly state the topic and the writer's position on the topic.**

Directly responding to the essay prompt

Option 1

1. Distribute copies of the prompts and theses (see below).
2. Instruct students to work individually and match the thesis with the prompt.
3. In pairs, have students compare and discuss reasons for their results.
4. Elicit answers.

Option 2

1. Distribute copies of the prompts and theses (see below).
2. Have students in pairs match the thesis with the prompt.
3. Elicit answers.

Prompt 1: Explain the most serious problem likely to be caused by rising affluence in China and recommend a solution to this problem.

Prompt 2: Examine the reasons why affluence is rising in China.

Prompt 3: Compare the rise of affluence in China with other developing Asian countries.

Prompt 4: Determine if lifestyles have changed in China due to rising affluence.

Prompt 5: Determine if affluence in China is having a more positive or negative effect on society.

Prompt 6: Discuss the possible future of China if it maintains its current rate of rising affluence.

Thesis a: With rising affluence, the Chinese have begun to adopt more Western standards in many parts of their life, but seem to have also kept many of their country's traditions.

Thesis b: Rising affluence in China is likely to lead to periods of increased competition, crime, and eventually self-reflection among members of a society so focused on earning as much money as possible.

Thesis c: Rising affluence in China is due in great part to its labor force and government policies.

Thesis d: Rising affluence in China has been quick and dramatic compared to development in countries such as Vietnam and the Philippines.

Thesis e: One very critical issue seems to owe its existence to rising affluence in China: a singular focus on making money at the expense of compassion for others. Therefore, education should focus on ensuring that children learn the value of community for the benefit of society.

Thesis f: Rising affluence in China is improving conditions for those who may consider themselves middle class, but it is also causing great harm to the environment.

(Answers)
1. e, 2. c, 3. d, 4. a, 5. f, 6. b

Option 3

1. Have students read the explanation and examples in the textbook.
2. Then, with books closed, have students in pairs or small groups summarize what they read.
3. Elicit answers to the question:
   - *How can you ensure your thesis is suitable?*
     (Answer: **Check the instructional wording in the essay prompt**.)

Emphasize:
- *Make sure your thesis matches the instructional words in the essay prompt.*

Exercise 1

Option 1

1. Have students work individually to complete the exercise.

2. When done, have students compare answers with a partner.

   NOTE: Have students also discuss why the other answers are less suitable.

3. Elicit answers.

Option 2

1. Divide the class into pairs or small groups.

2. Have students work collaboratively to complete the exercise.

   NOTE: Have students also discuss why the other answers are less suitable.

3. Elicit answers.

Section 2   Making an outline

Option 1

1. Elicit answers to the question:
   - *Why is a map useful?*

2. Emphasize:
   - *Without a map, you can easily get lost and waste a lot of time. An outline is like a map for your essay. Without an outline, you could lose your way and waste a lot of time.*

Option 2

1. Write the following questions on the board:
   - *Why is making an outline helpful?*
   - *What should you include in an essay outline?*

2. Have students work in pairs or small groups to discuss the questions.

3. Elicit answers and write them on the board.

4. Confirm answers.
   (Answers)
   - **An outline helps the writer logically organize how he or she plans to support the thesis in the essay, and also helps the writer to stay focused while writing.**
   - **It should include the thesis, each main argument, and the supporting points for each.**

Option 3

1. Have students read the explanation and example in the textbook.

2. Then, with books closed, have students in pairs or small groups summarize what they read.

3. Elicit answers to the question:
   - *What should an essay outline include?*
     (Answer: **It should include the thesis, each main argument, and the supporting points for each.**)

Option 4

1. Reproduce the outline form in the textbook, page 21, on the board, but with lines instead of words.

OUTLINE

2. Have students work in pairs to try to remember which words go in each line.

Exercise 2

Option 1

1. Have students work individually to complete the exercise.

2. When done, have students compare answers with a partner.

3. Elicit answers.

Option 2

1. Divide the class into pairs or small groups.

2. Have students work collaboratively to complete the exercise.

3. Elicit answers.

   Emphasize:
   - *The completed outline for this exercise is a suitable amount of detail for any essay outline. The writer is now ready to start writing the essay.*

Section 3　Model essay

The model essay presents a chance to introduce elements of an effective academic essay, which are covered in more detail in the next unit.

Option 1

1. Have students read the essay prompt, then the title of the model essay.
2. As students are reading, write the following on the board:
   * *Why is this an effective title?*
   * *What is the writer's likely position in the essay?*
3. Have students work in pairs or small groups to discuss the questions.
4. Elicit answers and write them on the board.
5. Confirm answers.
   (Answers)
   * **Effective title – From the title, the reader can understand what the essay will be about and the writer's position.**
   * **Likely position – The writer seems to support the use of nuclear energy as an energy source.**

   Emphasize:
   * *In the U.S. and Canada, universities often ask for an original title, but in the U.K., universities normally want just the essay prompt above the introductory paragraph.*

Option 2

1. Follow Option 1 above.
2. Then have students read the introductory paragraph.
3. In pairs, with books closed, have students summarize what they read.
4. Elicit a summary from select students.

Option 3

1. Follow Option 1 or 2 above.
2. Then have students reread the thesis (last sentence of the introductory paragraph).
3. Have students in pairs or small groups discuss:
   * *Based on the thesis, what specific information do you expect to read about in the rest of the essay?*
   (Possible answer: **amount of power from nuclear energy, comparison with other energy sources, data on environmental impact**)

Option 4

1. Follow Option 1, 2, or 3 above.
2. Then have students read the rest of the essay paragraph by paragraph.
3. Have students pause after each paragraph and summarize with a partner or in small groups what they read.
4. Elicit a summary from select students.

Option 5

1. Have students read the entire essay.
2. Then, with books closed, have students in pairs or small groups summarize what they read.
3. Elicit a summary from select students.

Option 6

1. Write the following on the board:
   * *Was the essay convincing?*
   * *Yes – 3　2　1　0 – No*
2. Have students in pairs or small groups discuss the question and pick a number reflecting their feeling.
3. Elicit answers plus reasons.
   (Possible answer)
   For me, the essay was a 2.5. Most of the arguments and evidence presented were convincing in supporting the idea that nuclear energy is relatively safe and really the only viable means of supplying the world's energy needs at this moment.

   The only criticism is that the argument for the safety of nuclear energy, which seems to be the chief concern of nuclear power critics, would have been stronger if it included more details about how the reactors themselves are safeguarded from catastrophic accidents. Simply comparing the number of fatalities between nuclear energy with those from coal and hydropower is not convincing, as likely the majority of deaths from extracting coal were from working in mines, and the majority of deaths from hydropower were the construction of dams and other facilities. The potential for death from a nuclear accident is not just to workers in a plant, but to those living in the surrounding area as well, as the accidents in Fukushima and Chernobyl showed.

Exercise 3

NOTE: This exercise is potentially time-consuming. The options below can be done with a few paragraphs instead of the whole essay.

Option 1

1. Have students work individually to complete the exercise.
2. When done, have students compare answers with a partner.
3. Elicit answers.

Option 2

1. Divide the class into pairs or small groups.
2. Have students work collaboratively to complete the exercise.
3. Elicit answers.

Option 3

1. Follow steps one and two of Option 2 above.

2. Re-divide students into new pairs or groups so they are sitting with at least one new person.

3. Have them compare answers with each other.

4. Elicit answers.

Option 4

1. Follow Option 1, 2, or 3 above.

2. Write the following on the board:
   - *How much of the essay replies to any of the four parts of the essay prompt?*

3. Have students work in pairs or small groups to discuss the question.

4. Elicit answers.

5. Confirm answer. (Answer: **The entire essay focuses on answering the four parts of the essay prompt – i.e., all of the points are relevant.**)

Option 1

1. Have students reread the introductory paragraph of the model essay on nuclear energy on page 24.

2. As students are reading, write the following questions on the board:
   - *Is the introductory paragraph effective? Why or why not?*

3. Then, with books closed, have students in pairs or small groups discuss the questions.

4. Elicit answers and write them on the board.

5. Confirm answer. (Answer: **It is effective because it introduces the topic and gives background on it to help prepare readers for the rest of the essay.**)

Option 2

1. Write the following on the board:
   - *What is the purpose of the introductory paragraph?*

2. Have students work in pairs or small groups to discuss the question.

3. Elicit answers and write them on the board.

4. Confirm answer. (Answer: **To introduce the essay topic and prepare readers for the contents of the essay.**)

5. Then write the following on the board:
   - *Is it better to write your introductory paragraph before or after writing the rest of the essay?*

6. Have students work in pairs or small groups to discuss the question.

7. Elicit answers and write them on the board.

8. Confirm answer.
   (Answer)
   When to write introductory paragraph:
   Before rest of essay –
   - **natural to write the introductory paragraph first, since it is the first paragraph of the essay**
   - **may help keep the writer focused when writing the rest of the essay**

   After rest of essay –
   - **helps ensure the introductory paragraph's contents match the contents of the essay**
   - **writer will know better what background information to include in the introductory paragraph to help readers understand the rest of the essay**

Option 3

1. Have students read the explanation in the textbook on page 32, but stop before they get to "Section 1 – What to include."

2. As students are reading, write the following questions on the board:
   - *What is the purpose of the introductory paragraph?*
   - *Is it better to write your introductory paragraph before or after writing the rest of the essay?*

3. Then, with books closed, have students in pairs or small groups discuss the questions.

4. Elicit answers and write them on the board.

5. Confirm answers.
   (Answers)
   Introductory paragraph purpose – to introduce the essay topic and prepare readers for the contents of the essay

   When to write introductory paragraph:
   Before rest of essay –
   - **natural to write the introductory paragraph first, since it is the first paragraph of the essay**
   - **may help keep the writer focused when writing the rest of the essay**

   After rest of essay –
   - **helps ensure the introductory paragraph's contents match the contents of the essay**
   - **writer will know better what background information to include in the introductory paragraph to help readers understand the rest of the essay**

   Emphasize:
   - *The thesis is the most important sentence in the essay, so this should be the first part of the essay written.*
   - *If you choose to also write the entire introductory paragraph before the rest of the essay, do not spend too much time on it. The contents may have to be changed after writing the rest of the essay.*

Section 1 What to include

1. Background on the topic

Option 1

1. Have students look again at the introductory paragraph of the model essay on nuclear energy on page 24 and answer this question:
   - *What kind of background information is given?*
2. Elicit answers and write them on the board.
3. Confirm answers.
   (Answers)
   Statistics – nuclear power 13.4% of world's energy supply, 301 new reactors under construction

   Current situation – growing population, need to curb dependence on fossil fuels

   Different perspectives – Others, wary of the potential risks of nuclear power . . .

Option 2

1. Have students read the explanations and example in the textbook on pages 32–33.
2. As students are reading, write the following questions on the board:
   - *What should the introductory paragraph include?*
   - *What background information could be helpful in an introductory paragraph?*
3. Elicit answers and write them on the board.
4. Confirm answers.
   (Answers)
   - **The introductory paragraph should include background on the topic, the writer's thesis, and a motive for the essay.**
   - **Helpful background information could be a history of the topic, the current situation, different perspectives, definitions of key terms, statistics.**

> **Exercise 1**

Option 1

1. Have students work individually to complete the exercise.
2. When done, have students compare answers with a partner.
3. Elicit answers.

Option 2

1. Divide the class into pairs or small groups.
2. Have students work collaboratively to complete the exercise.
3. Elicit answers.

Selecting background to include

Option 1

1. Write the following question on the board:
   - *How do you decide what background information to include in the introductory paragraph?*
2. Have students work in pairs or small groups to discuss the question.
3. Elicit answers and write them on the board.
4. Confirm answer.
   (Answer)
   Deciding on what background information to include depends on understanding the knowledge of the potential readers. For example:
   - **Readers less knowledgeable on the topic will need more basic information.**
   - **Readers fairly knowledgeable on the topic should be presented with information which is new and may even challenge what they currently know or assume.**

Option 2

1. Follow Option 1 above.
2. Have students read the explanation and examples in the textbook.
3. Then, with books closed, have students in pairs or small groups summarize what they read.
4. Elicit answers to the question:
   What is the key question you should ask when deciding what background information to include? (Answer: **What background information is necessary for readers to understand the essay contents?**)

> **Exercise 2**

NOTE: Encourage students to write specific details rather than the general types of background information listed on page 32 of the textbook.

Option 1

1. Have students work individually to complete the exercise.
2. When done, have students compare answers with a partner.
3. Elicit answers.

Option 2

1. Divide the class into pairs or small groups.
2. Have students work collaboratively to complete the exercise.
3. Elicit answers.

Option 3

1. Follow steps one and two of Option 2 above.

2. Re-divide students into new pairs or groups so they are sitting with at least one new person.

3. Have them compare answers with each other.

4. Elicit answers.

2. The writer's thesis

Option 1

1. Elicit answers to the following questions:
   - *What is the thesis?*
   - *Where does the thesis often appear?*

2. Confirm answers. (Answers: **The thesis is a clear statement of the writer's position on the topic. It is often the last sentence of the introductory paragraph.**)

Option 2

1. Have students read the explanation and example in the textbook.

2. Quickly elicit:
   - *What is the thesis?*
   - *Where does the thesis often appear?*

3. Confirm answers. (Answers: **The thesis is a clear statement of the writer's position on the topic. It is often the last sentence of the introductory paragraph.**)

   Emphasize:
   - *The essay should focus on supporting the thesis.*

3. A motive for the essay

Option 1

1. Introduce the idea of a motive for the essay by writing the following theses on the board:
   - *A comparison between the American and Malaysian primary school education systems reveals why math and science are more highly regarded by students in Asia than in North America.*
   - *It seems apparent that with improvements in medical technology, the average lifespan of humans will increase.*

2. Then, below the theses, write this question on the board:
   - *If either thesis was the first sentence in an essay, what would you think?*

3. Have students work in pairs or small groups to discuss the question.

4. Elicit answers and write them on the board.

5. Confirm answer.
   (Answer)
   A reader might think "So what!" after reading each thesis. The reader would not understand the need for the thesis. For example:
   - **The first thesis comparing the American and Malaysian education systems begs the question, "Why compare these two particular systems?"**

- **The second thesis seems obvious, so it is not clear what the reader would gain from reading an essay supporting it.**

6. Emphasize:
   - *While a thesis is necessary to tell readers what the essay will contain, a motive is necessary to tell readers the value of the essay – i.e., it explains, "Why is the issue worth exploring or debating?"*

7. Write the following possible motives on the board.
   - *Possible motive for thesis 1:*
     While nearly 25 percent of American elementary school students view math and science as dry, boring academic subjects, their Malaysian peers are nearly the opposite, with more than 75 percent regarding math and science as interesting.
   - *Possible motive for thesis 2:*
     Of course, medical discoveries since the middle of the nineteenth century have helped increase the average lifespan, but more recent discoveries have researchers predicting future life spans of 500 years or longer.

8. Also inform students:
   For thesis 2, the problem was that the thesis is too obvious. A change to make the thesis less obvious could be:
   - *It seems apparent that with improvements in medical technology, the average lifespan of humans will ~~increase~~ potentially be limitless.*

Option 2

1. Have students read the explanation and examples in the textbook.

2. As students are reading, write the following questions on the board:
   - *What is a motive?*
   - *What are three common motives for an academic essay?*

3. Have students work in pairs or small groups to discuss the questions.

4. Elicit answers and write them on the board.

5. Confirm answers.
   (Answers)
   - **A motive is the reason why it is necessary to take a certain position on a topic or why the topic is worth exploring.**
   - **Three common types of motives are:**
     - **There is an issue worthy of debate.**
     - **There is a problem requiring a solution or explanation.**
     - **There is information which may aid understanding.**

Exercise 3

Option 1

1. Have students work individually to complete the exercise.
2. When done, have students compare answers with a partner.
3. Elicit answers.

Option 2

1. Divide the class into pairs.
2. Have students work collaboratively to complete the exercise.
3. Elicit answers.

Exercise 4

Option 1

1. Have students work individually to complete the exercise.
2. When done, have students compare answers with a partner.
3. Elicit answers.

Option 2

1. Divide the class into pairs.
2. Have students work collaboratively to complete the exercise.
3. Elicit answers.

Exercise 5

Option 1

1. Have students work individually to complete the exercise.
2. When done, have students compare answers with a partner.

   NOTE: Also have students identify which kind of motivating point their partner wrote.
3. Elicit answers.

Option 2

1. Divide the class into pairs or small groups.
2. Have students work collaboratively to complete the exercise.
3. Elicit answers.

Option 3

1. Follow steps one and two of Option 2 above.
2. Re-divide students into new pairs or groups so they are sitting with at least one new person.
3. Have them compare answers with each other.

   NOTE: Also have students identify which kind of motivating point the other students wrote.
4. Elicit answers.

UNIT 2

Part 2
Body paragraphs

Purpose and parts

Option 1

1. Elicit answers to the following questions:
   - *What is the purpose of body paragraphs?*
   - *What three parts do body paragraphs often have?*
2. Confirm answers.
   (Answers)
   - **Body paragraphs present details in a logical order to help support the thesis.**
   - **Body paragraphs often have a topic sentence, supporting sentences, and an optional transitional sentence.**

Option 2

1. Have students read the explanation in the textbook but stop before they get to "Section 1 – Topic sentences."
2. Elicit answers to the following questions:
   - *What is the purpose of body paragraphs?*
   - *What three parts do body paragraphs often have?*
3. Confirm answers.
   (Answers)
   - **Body paragraphs present details in a logical order to help support the thesis.**
   - **They often have a topic sentence, supporting sentences, and an optional transitional sentence.**

Section 1   Topic sentences

Option 1

1. Write the following sentences on the board:
   - *No guarantee of employment or a desired salary is another reason it is not worth it.*
   - *Status is one perceived benefit.*
2. Then, below the sentences, write this question:
   - *If either of these were the first sentence of a paragraph, what would be the problem?*

   NOTE: Alternatively, instead of the above question, write:
   - *If either of these were the first sentence of a paragraph,*
   - *would you know the thesis of the essay?*
   - *would you know what the paragraph contents would be?*
3. Have students work in pairs or small groups to discuss the question.
4. Elicit answers and write them on the board.

5. Confirm answers.
   (Answers)
   - **Neither the topic nor the thesis is clear.**
   - **It is not clear what the paragraph will be about.**

Option 2

1. Have students read the explanation and examples in the textbook on page 42.
2. As students are reading, write the following questions on the board:
   - *What is the purpose of a topic sentence?*
   - *What should a topic sentence include?*
   - *What should you keep in mind when writing a topic sentence?*
3. Have students work in pairs or small groups to discuss the questions.
4. Elicit answers and write them on the board.
5. Confirm answers.
   (Answers)
   A topic sentence should state what the body paragraph will be about.
   It should include the topic and controlling idea – the idea the paragraph should be focused on supporting.
   When wording a topic sentence:
   - **It may start with either the topic or the controlling idea.**
   - **Precise words should be used, while pronouns and general words should be avoided.**

   Emphasize:
   - *Upon reading the topic sentence, the reader should understand what the paragraph will be about.*
   - *Restating the topic and position from the thesis in the topic sentence shows the reader how the paragraph is related to the essay's goal.*

Exercise 1

Option 1

1. Have students work individually to complete the exercise.
2. When done, have students compare answers with a partner.
3. Elicit answers.

Option 2

1. Divide the class into pairs or small groups.
2. Have students work collaboratively to complete the exercise.
3. Elicit answers.

Relevance

Option 1

1. Have students read the explanation and example in the textbook on page 43.

2. Quickly elicit:
   - *What should a writer pay attention to when writing a topic sentence?*

3. Confirm answer. (Answer: **The writer should make sure the topic sentence shows relevance to the essay thesis.**)

Option 2

1. Follow Option 1 above.

2. Then have students look again at the example essay prompt on reality TV shows and discuss in pairs or small groups:
   - *What key words in the essay prompt tell the writer whether or not a topic sentence is relevant?*

3. Elicit answers.

4. Confirm answers. (Answer: **reality TV, American character/preferences**)

Exercise 2

Option 1

1. Have students work individually to complete the exercise.

2. When done, have students compare answers with a partner.

3. Elicit answers.

Option 2

1. Divide the class into pairs or small groups.

2. Have students work collaboratively to complete the exercise.

3. Elicit answers.

Section 2 | Supporting sentences and the "waltz"

Option 1

1. Have students read the explanation in the textbook on page 45, but stop before getting to the examples.

2. As students are reading, write the following on the board:
   - *How should supporting sentences be similar to "the waltz"?*
   - *What are the three parts of the paragraph "waltz"?*

3. Have students work in pairs or small groups to discuss the questions.

4. Elicit answers.

5. Confirm answers.
   (Answers)
   - **Ordering supporting sentences should follow three steps, just like the waltz.**
   - **claim, evidence, explanation**

Option 2

1. Have students read the explanation under "Examples, a, Part 1: Body paragraph developing . . ." in the textbook, page 45.

2. As students are reading, write the following question on the board:
   - *How does the claim support the topic sentence?*

3. Have students work in pairs or small groups to discuss the question.

4. Elicit answers and write them on the board.

5. Confirm answer. (Answer: **According to the claim, the introduction of photographs led many painters to switch subject matter in their paintings from people of status or landscapes to regular people.**)

6. Then write this question on the board:
   - *Why is this claim not enough to convince a reader?*

7. Have students work in pairs or small groups to discuss the question.

8. Elicit answers and write them on the board.

9. Confirm answer. (Answer: **Without evidence, readers are asked to trust that what the writer is claiming is true. Unless the writer is a renowned expert on the topic, readers have no reason to trust what the writer is claiming.**)

Option 3

1. Have students read "Examples, b, Part 2: Evidence added . . ." in the textbook, page 46.

2. As students are reading, write the following question on the board:
   - *How does the evidence support the claim?*

3. Have students work in pairs or small groups to discuss the question.

4. Elicit answers and write them on the board.

5. Confirm answer. (Answer: **The evidence gives examples of paintings depicting everyday life – a rainy street scene – as subject matter.**)

6. Then write this question on the board:
   - *Why is this evidence not enough to complete the argument?*

7. Have students work in pairs or small groups to discuss the question.

8. Elicit answers and write them on the board.

9. Confirm answer. (Answer: **The evidence by itself is just a reporting of facts. Readers are asked to interpret the significance of this evidence in terms of the history of art. The writer should provide an explanation of this significance.**)

Option 4

1. Have students read "Examples, c, Part 3: Explanation added . . ." in the textbook, page 46.

2. As students are reading, write the following question on the board:
    *   *How does the explanation help the reader understand the significance of the claim and evidence?*

3. Have students work in pairs or small groups to discuss the question.

4. Elicit answers and write them on the board.

5. Confirm answer. (Answer: **The switch was a "revolution" where ordinary people were now considered worthy subjects of art.**)

6. Then write this question on the board:
    *   *Is this waltz enough to show why the topic sentence is true?*

7. Have students work in pairs or small groups to discuss the question.

8. Elicit answers and write them on the board.

9. Confirm answer. (Answer: **Perhaps, but very often multiple "waltz" patterns appear in a paragraph or over several paragraphs to support one topic sentence.**)

10. Have students read "e. Body paragraphs with multiple claims" in the textbook, page 48.

11. Elicit:
    *   *What was the controlling idea in the topic sentence?*

12. Confirm answer. (Answer: **The mass production of cameras made society more equal.**)

13. Then elicit:
    *   *What claims did the writer make to support this?*

14. Confirm answer. (Answer: **1. Cameras became cheaper, meaning many more people could afford to buy one; and 2. The inexpensive "snapshot" allowed almost everyone to be able to record the events of their life.**)

15. Then elicit:
    *   *Why is having multiple waltzes useful?*

16. Confirm answer. (Answer: **While a single waltz is strong, a multiple waltz is even stronger if a point can be supported from a variety of angles using a variety of evidence.**)

Option 5

1. Have students read "Examples, d, Parts 2 and 3; Reversed position . . ." in the textbook, page 47.

2. Emphasize:
    *   *The paragraph "waltz" does not necessarily have to follow a 1 – 2 – 3 order. It could be 1 – 3 – 2, 1 – 2 – 2 – 3, etc. Basically, it is recommended that writers have all three parts to be sure the topic sentence is adequately supported.*

Emphasize:
*   *When writing body paragraphs, the key thing is to explain each claim using these three steps. This ensures ideas are clearly explained and fully developed. Without these three steps, the writer's ideas may be misinterpreted or ineffective.*
*   *One way to view the waltz pattern is:*
    Topic sentence
    ① ***One reason is*** *. . . (reason supporting the topic sentence).*
    ② ***For example,*** *. . . (evidence supporting the claim).*
    ③ ***Therefore,*** *. . . (why the claim and evidence are important – what they mean).*

Exercise 3

NOTE: This exercise may prove time-consuming and/ or challenging. One option is to provide one or two answers as hints.

Option 1

1. Have students work individually to complete the exercise.

2. When done, have students compare answers with a partner.

3. Elicit answers.

Option 2

1. Divide the class into pairs or small groups.

2. Have students work collaboratively to complete the exercise.

3. Elicit answers.

Exercise 4

Do the items one at a time and follow any option below. Doing both items in a row without an answer check may be difficult for students.

Option 1

1. Have students work individually to complete the exercise.

2. When done, have students compare answers with a partner.

3. Elicit answers.

Option 2

1. Divide the class into pairs or small groups.

2. Have students work collaboratively to complete the exercise.

3. Elicit answers.

Option 3

1. Follow steps one and two of Option 2 above.

2. Re-divide students into new pairs or groups so they are sitting with at least one new person.

3. Have them compare answers with each other.

4. Elicit answers.

Exercise 5

Do the items one at a time and follow any option below. Doing both items in a row without an answer check may be difficult for students.

Option 1

1. Have students work individually to complete the exercise.
2. When done, have students compare answers with a partner.
3. Elicit answers.

Option 2

1. Divide the class into pairs or small groups.
2. Have students work collaboratively to complete the exercise.
3. Elicit answers.

Option 3

1. Follow steps one and two of Option 2 above.
2. Re-divide students into new pairs or groups so they are sitting with at least one new person.
3. Have them compare answers with each other.
4. Elicit answers.

Section 3 Transitional sentences

Option 1

1. Elicit answers to these questions:
   - *What is the purpose of a transitional sentence?*
   - *What are examples of transitional words or phrases?*
2. Confirm answers.
   (Answers)
   - **A transitional sentence prepares readers for some change [transition] upcoming in the essay.**
   - **Common examples of transitional words or phrases are** *however, therefore, furthermore, for example.*

Option 2

1. Have students read the explanation and examples in the textbook, page 52.
2. As students are reading, write the following questions on the board:
   - *Why are transitional sentences useful?*
   - *Where might a transitional sentence appear in a paragraph?*
3. Elicit answers and write them on the board.
4. Confirm answers.
   (Answers)
   - **Transitional sentences can prepare readers for a change in ideas, or add emphasis to the new idea.**
   - **A transitional sentence can appear at the end or at the beginning of a paragraph.**

Section 4 Body paragraphs without topic sentences

Option 1

1. Elicit answers to this question:
   - *Why is it possible for a paragraph to not have a topic sentence?*
2. Confirm answer. (Answer: **A paragraph without a topic sentence may continue to support the topic sentence of the previous paragraph.**)

Option 2

1. Have students read the explanation and example in the textbook, page 53.
2. Elicit answers to this question:
   - *Why is it possible for a paragraph to not have a topic sentence?*
3. Confirm answer. (Answer: **A paragraph without a topic sentence may continue to support the topic sentence of the previous paragraph.**)

Exercise 6

Have students read and complete the three tasks one body paragraph at a time. Doing the entire essay without an answer check may be difficult for students.

Option 1

1. Have students work individually to complete the exercise.
2. When done, have students compare their answers with a partner.
3. Elicit answers.

Option 2

1. Divide the class into pairs or small groups.
2. Have students work collaboratively to complete the exercise.
3. Elicit answers.

UNIT 2

Part 3
Logical fallacies

To introduce the concept of logical fallacies:

1. Write the following on the board:
   - *The U.S. is dangerous because they allow guns.*
   - *If you do not get a university education, life will be difficult.*
   - *People support the military because they like war.*
   - *People should visit the Great Wall of China because it is a UNESCO World Heritage Site.*
   - *Are these points logical? Why or why not?*

2. Have students work in pairs or small groups to discuss the question at the end.

3. Elicit answers and write them on the board.

4. Confirm answer.
   (Answer)
   The points have some problems with logic. For example:
   - **The first point about the U.S. and guns is a possible example of a false cause – other countries such as Canada allow guns, but the crime rate there is far lower than in the U.S.**
   - **The point about university education can be an example of a false dichotomy.**
   - **The point about supporting the military can be an example of a straw man.**
   - **The point about the Great Wall can be an example of false appeal.**

   Emphasize:
   - *Although there are many ways for arguments to be illogical, logical fallacies generally fall into two categories: overgeneralization and irrelevance.*

Section 1 Overgeneralization

Option 1

1. Have students read the explanation and examples in the textbook, pages 60–61.

2. As students are reading, write the following questions on the board:
   - *What is the fallacy of division?*
   - *What is a false cause?*
   - *What is a false dichotomy?*

3. Then, with books closed, have students in pairs or small groups discuss the questions.

4. Elicit answers and write them on the board.

5. Confirm answers.
   (Answers)
   - **Fallacy of division – small sample applied to whole group**
   - **False cause – cause is not/cannot be proven**
   - **False dichotomy – only two options presented when more than two actually exist**

Option 2

1. Divide the class into groups of three.

2. Have each student in a group read one of the overgeneralization fallacies in the textbook, pages 60–61.

3. As students are reading, write the following questions on the board:
   - *What is the fallacy of division?*
   - *What is a false cause?*
   - *What is a false dichotomy?*

4. Then, with books closed, have each student explain his or her fallacy to the other group members and give the example presented in the book.

5. Elicit answers and write them on the board.

6. Confirm answers.
   (Answers)
   - **Fallacy of division – small sample applied to whole group**
   - **False cause – cause is not/cannot be proven**
   - **False dichotomy – only two options presented when more than two actually exist**

Exercise 1

Have students read and complete the three paragraphs one at a time. Doing all three paragraphs in a row without an answer check may be difficult for students.

Option 1

1. Have students work individually to complete the exercise.

2. When done, have students compare answers with a partner.

3. Elicit answers.

Option 2

1. Divide the class into pairs or small groups.

2. Have students work collaboratively to complete the exercise.

3. Elicit answers.

Section 2 Irrelevance

Option 1

1. Have students read the explanation and examples of the first two fallacies under "Irrelevance" in the textbook, pages 62–63.

2. As students are reading, write the following questions on the board:
   - *What is a straw man?*
   - *What is a slippery slope?*
   - *What is a false appeal?*
   - *What is circular reasoning?*
   - *What is non-sequitur?*

3. Then, with books closed, have students in pairs or small groups discuss the first two questions.

4. Elicit answers and write them on the board.

5. Confirm answers.
   (Answers)
   - **Straw man – opposing side represented inaccurately to easily argue against it**
   - **Slippery slope – one cause will lead to a chain of events**

6. Have students read the explanation and examples of the last three fallacies in the textbook, pages 63–64.

7. Then, with books closed, have students in pairs or small groups discuss the answers to the last three questions in step two.

8. Elicit answers and write them on the board.

9. Confirm answers.
   (Answers)
   - **False appeal – unrelated authority or reason used to support an argument**
   - **Circular reasoning – conclusion is same as original argument**
   - **Non-sequitur – no/weak connection between reason and conclusion**

Option 2

1. Divide the class into groups of five.

2. Have each student in a group read one of the irrelevance fallacies on pages 62–64.

3. As students are reading, write the following questions on the board:
   - *What is a straw man?*
   - *What is a slippery slope?*
   - *What is a false appeal?*
   - *What is circular reasoning?*
   - *What is non-sequitur?*

4. Then, with books closed, have each student explain his or her fallacy to the other group members and give the example presented in the book.

5. Elicit answers and write them on the board.

6. Confirm answers.
   (Answers)
   - **Straw man – opposing side represented inaccurately to easily argue against it**
   - **Slippery slope – one cause will lead to a chain of events**
   - **False appeal – unrelated authority or reason used to support an argument**
   - **Circular reasoning – conclusion is same as original argument**
   - **Non-sequitur – no/weak connection between reason and conclusion**

Exercise 2

Have students read and complete the five paragraphs one at a time. Doing all five paragraphs in a row without an answer check may be difficult for students.

Option 1

1. Have students work individually to complete the exercise.

2. When done, have students compare answers with a partner.

3. Elicit answers.

Option 2

1. Divide the class into pairs or small groups.

2. Have students work collaboratively to complete the exercise.

3. Elicit answers.

Exercise 3

Have students read and complete each item one at a time. Doing all of the items in a row without an answer check may be difficult for students.

Option 1

1. Have students work individually to complete the exercise.

2. When done, have students compare answers with a partner.

3. Elicit answers.

Option 2

1. Divide the class into pairs or small groups.

2. Have students work collaboratively to complete the exercise.

3. Elicit answers.

2 | Part 4
Concluding paragraphs

Option 1

1. Write the following on the board:
   * *What should a concluding paragraph do?*
2. Have students work in pairs or small groups to discuss the question.
3. Elicit answers and write them on the board.
4. Confirm answer. (Answer: **The concluding paragraph should tell readers that the essay is coming to a close by reminding readers of the essay's thesis and main points from each body paragraph, and by giving readers a final thought regarding the topic.**)

Option 2

1. Have students reread the concluding paragraph of the model essay on nuclear energy on page 27.
2. As students are reading, write the following question on the board:
   * *Why is this concluding paragraph effective?*
3. Have students work in pairs or small groups to discuss the question.
4. Elicit answers and write them on the board.
5. Confirm answer. (Answer: **The concluding paragraph in the model essay is effective because it reminds readers of the essay's thesis and main points from each body paragraph, and it gives readers a final thought regarding the topic.**)

Option 3

1. Have students read the explanation and example in the textbook on page 69, but stop before reading "Section 1 – An effective final thought."
2. As students are reading, write the following question on the board:
   * *What should a concluding paragraph do?*
3. Then, with books closed, have students in pairs or small groups discuss the question.
4. Elicit answers and write them on the board.
5. Confirm answer. (Answer: **The concluding paragraph should tell readers that the essay is coming to a close by reminding readers of the essay's thesis and main points from each body paragraph, and by giving readers a final thought regarding the topic.**)

Section 1 | An effective final thought

Option 1

1. Have students read the explanation and examples in the textbook, page 70.
2. As students are reading, write the following question on the board:
   * *What are some ways to write an effective final thought?*
3. Then, with books closed, have students in pairs or small groups discuss the question.
4. Elicit answers and write them on the board.
5. Confirm answer.
   (Answer)
   * **Re-emphasize the importance of the issue or the position taken.**
   * **Make a prediction based on the facts.**
   * **Make a recommendation for further action.**
   * **Assess the value of the arguments in the essay.**

Option 2

1. Have students reread the final two sentences in the concluding paragraph of the model essay on nuclear energy on page 27.
2. As students are reading, write the following question on the board:
   * *Why is this final thought effective?*
3. Have students work in pairs or small groups to discuss the question.
4. Elicit answers and write them on the board.
5. Confirm answer. (Answer: **It makes a prediction about renewable energies [that they will eventually provide adequate power], but it also makes a recommendation for further action [the government and nuclear agencies should inform the public more aggressively about the benefits of nuclear power].**)

Section 2 | What to avoid in the concluding paragraph

Option 1

1. Have students read the explanation and examples in the textbook, page 70.
2. As students are reading, write the following question on the board:
   * *What is not suitable in a concluding paragraph?*
3. Then, with books closed, have students in pairs or small groups discuss the question.

4. Elicit answers and write them on the board.

5. Confirm answer.
   (Answer)
   • **New information**
   • **Empty statements**

Option 2

1. Follow Option 1 above.

2. Then elicit answers to the following:
   • *What examples are given in the textbook regarding Antarctica?*

3. With books closed, have students in pairs or small groups try to recall the examples given.

4. Elicit and confirm answer.
   (Answer)
   • **Global warming is sure to increase if nothing is done to protect Antarctica.**
   • **The evidence shows that tourism in Antarctica is a difficult problem.**
   • **Nature is a precious resource that is important for everyone.**

Exercise 1

Have students read and complete each item one at a time. Doing all of the items in a row without an answer check may be difficult for students.

Option 1

1. Have students work individually to complete the exercise.

2. When done, have students compare answers with a partner.

3. Elicit answers.

Option 2

1. Divide the class into pairs or small groups.

2. Have students work collaboratively to complete the exercise.

3. Elicit answers.

Option 3

1. Follow steps one and two of Option 2 above.

2. Re-divide students into new pairs or groups so they are sitting with at least one new person.

3. Have them compare answers with each other.

4. Elicit answers.

To introduce the topic:

Option 1

1. Write the following on the board:
   * *What is the problem with an essay that does not use information from sources?*

2. Have students work in pairs or small groups to discuss the question.

3. Elicit answers and write them on the board.

4. Confirm answer. (Answer: **An essay without information from sources is basically a presentation of the writer's own information and ideas. This begs the question, "Why should readers trust what the writer is saying?")**

Option 2

1. Follow Option 1 above.

2. Then write the following on the board:
   * *When you use information from sources, what else do you need to do?*
   * *Why is it necessary to do this?*

   OR

   * *Why is it necessary to show when you have taken information from outside sources?*

3. Have students work in pairs or small groups to discuss the questions.

4. Elicit answers and write them on the board.

5. Confirm answers.
   (Answers)
   * **When using information from sources, you need to give credit to the original sources by citing them.**
   * **Not doing so is plagiarism – presenting someone else's ideas as your own = stealing.**

Option 3

1. Follow Option 1 or 2 above.

2. Then write the following on the board:
   * *Why do some students plagiarize?*

3. Have students work in pairs or small groups to discuss the question.

4. Elicit answers and write them on the board.

5. Confirm answer.
   (Answer)
   Students plagiarize because:
   * **they are overwhelmed and are in a rush to write the essay before the deadline.**
   * **they did not know that taking others' ideas without citing is wrong.**
   * **they know it is wrong but think the professor will not catch them.**
   * **they are lazy and do not care whether or not the professor catches them.**

Emphasize:

* *It is tempting to simply "cut and paste" whole ideas from a source into an essay. However, doing so carelessly often results in plagiarizing, which in academic settings is taken seriously. Students can be expelled for doing it. However, it can be avoided by following a few techniques.*
* *In English-speaking countries, an important aspect of education is showing that you understand other people's ideas and you can respond to them. Simply copying information is not regarded as a high-level academic skill. Therefore, as well as avoiding plagiarism, the successful use of citation helps students to achieve high grades.*

Section 1 | Primary, secondary, and tertiary sources

Option 1

1. Write the following on the board:
   * *Research from Los Angeles University shows that 90% of Americans reported having been the victim of some kind of crime. You read about the study in the magazine <u>American Lifestyle</u>.*
   * *If you were going to use the information from this research in your essay, which source would you cite?*

2. Have students work in pairs or small groups to discuss the question.

3. Elicit answers and write them on the board.

4. Confirm answer.
   (Answer)
   * **Los Angeles University is the "primary source" – where the information originally came from.**
   * ***American Lifestyle* is the "secondary source" – which reported the research study.**
   * **As much as possible, the primary source should be cited, even if the writer originally found the information in a secondary source. This requires going to the primary source [website or journal], checking and confirming the research results.**

Option 2

1. Have students read the explanations in the textbook, pages 74–75.

2. As students are reading, write the following question on the board:
   * *What is the difference between a primary, secondary, and tertiary source?*

3. Then, with books closed, have students in pairs or small groups discuss the question.

4. Elicit answers and write them on the board.

5. Confirm answer.
(Answer)
   - **Primary – where information originally comes from**
   - **Secondary – reports/interprets information from primary sources**
   - **Tertiary – collects information from primary and secondary sources and presents in a condensed description**

Exercise 1

Option 1

1. Have students work individually to complete the exercise.

2. When done, have students compare answers with a partner.

3. Elicit answers.

Option 2

1. Divide the class into pairs or small groups.

2. Have students work collaboratively to complete the exercise.

3. Elicit answers.

Section 2 Determining credibility

Option 1

1. Write the following on the board:
   - *The Society for the Prevention of Aging reported that taking vitamin supplements daily may extend your life.*
   - *What questions should you ask to determine how much you can trust this information?*

2. Have students work in pairs or small groups to discuss the question.

3. Elicit answers and write them on the board.

4. Confirm answer.
   (Example answer)
   Determine:
   - **What is the reputation of the organization?**
   - **What is the goal of the organization?**
   - **When was the information originally published?**
   - **What is the report based on?**

Option 2

1. Have students read the explanations in the textbook.

2. As students are reading, write the following question on the board:
   - *How do you evaluate the credibility of information from a source?*

3. Then, with books closed, have students in pairs or small groups discuss the question.

4. Elicit answers and write them on the board.

5. Confirm answer. (Answer: **Ask questions regarding the author, publisher, purpose, accuracy, and context of the information.**)

Option 3

If students are in possession of a smartphone, or have immediate internet access via a computer:

1. Write the following on the board:
   - *Workplace accidents*
   - *Natural disasters*
   - *Best computer*
   - *Best place to work*
   - *Best university*

2. Then instruct students:
   - *Use your smartphone or computer and enter the first item from the list in a search engine (Google, Bing, Baidu, etc.).*
   - *Click on the first website which appears in the search results.*
   - *Discuss with a partner or in small groups: What does the website say about workplace accidents?*
   - *In pairs or small groups, determine if the information is credible.*

3. Elicit answers and write them on the board.

4. Repeat the process for the rest of the listed items on the board.

UNIT 3

Part 2
Integrating source information

Section 1 — Paraphrasing, summarizing, and quoting

Option 1

1. Write the following on the board:
   - *What is the difference between paraphrasing, summarizing, and quoting?*
   - *Why are they necessary when using information from outside sources?*
2. Have students work in pairs or small groups to discuss the questions.
3. Elicit answers and write them on the board.
4. Confirm answers.
   (Answers)
   - **Paraphrasing – specific details of source information written in writer's own words**
   - **Summarizing – main idea of source information is written in writer's own words in a condensed version**
   - **Quotation – words from source information are not changed and placed in quotation marks**

   They are necessary to avoid plagiarism.

Choosing to paraphrase or summarize

Option 1

1. Write the following on the board:
   - *Why not just cut and paste all source information and put them in quotes?*
2. Have students work in pairs or small groups to discuss the question.
3. Elicit answers and write them on the board.
4. Confirm answer.
   (Answer)
   - **Quoting should only be used when the exact wording has a high degree of impact on the reader.**
   - **Sometimes the exact words from the original source can be confusing, so paraphrasing or summarizing can make it easier for the reader to understand the source information.**
   - **Too many quotes in an essay make it seem like the whole essay is just someone else's words and ideas.**

Option 2 (Alternate to the two preceding Option 1s)

1. Have students read the explanations in the textbook, page 77, but stop before "Shared language."
2. As students are reading, write the following questions on the board:
   - *What is the difference between paraphrasing, summarizing, and quoting?*
   - *Why are they necessary when using information from outside sources?*
   - *Why would you choose to paraphrase or summarize?*
   - *How can you determine whether or not to paraphrase or summarize?*
3. Then, with books closed, have students in pairs or small groups discuss the first two questions.
4. Elicit answers and write them on the board.
5. Confirm answers.
   (Answers)
   - **Paraphrasing – specific details of source information written in writer's own words**
   - **Summarizing – main idea of source information is written in writer's own words in a condensed version**
   - **Quotation – words from source information are not changed and placed in quotation marks**

   They are necessary to avoid plagiarism.

6. Then have students in pairs or small groups discuss the last two questions.
7. Elicit answers and write them on the board.
8. Confirm answers.
   (Answers)
   - **Paraphrase or summarize when the exact wording of the original source information is not important, or even confusing.**
   - **If source information is <50 words, then paraphrase. Otherwise, summarize.**

Option 3

1. Have students read the explanations in the textbook, page 77, under Section 1, but stop before reading "Shared language."

2. As students are reading, draw the following table on the board:

	Definition	When to use
Quotation		
Paraphrasing		
Summarizing		

3. Then, with books closed, have students in pairs or small groups recall what they read.

4. Elicit answers to fill in the table.

	Definition	When to use
Quotation	words from source information are not changed and placed in quotation marks	when the exact wording of original has a strong impact on the reader NOTE: Students will not have read this, but try to elicit it anyway.
Paraphrasing	specific details of source information written in writer's own words	if source information is <50 words and exact wording of original is not important
Summarizing	main idea of source information is written in writer's own words in a condensed version	if source information is >50 words and exact wording of original is not important

Emphasize:
- *Use quoting when the original statement is powerfully or concisely worded.*
- *Use paraphrasing to give specific details from the source.*
- *Use summarizing only when the theme or main idea from a source is needed.*

Shared language

Option 1

1. Write the following on the board:
   - *The three sports with the most valuable teams in the world are soccer, American football, and baseball.*

2. Elicit:
   - *If paraphrasing this information, do you have to change every word?*

3. Confirm answer.
   (Answer)
   - **No, some words cannot or should not be changed because they are the most effective way to express something. This is called "shared language."**
   - **So the words "soccer," "American football," and "baseball" should not be changed. The rest of the words could and should be changed.**

Option 2

1. Have students read the explanation and examples in the textbook, page 78.

2. As students are reading, write the following questions on the board:
   - *What should you identify before writing a paraphrase or summary?*
   - *What are some examples of this?*

3. Then, with books closed, have students in pairs or small groups discuss the questions.

4. Elicit answers and write them on the board.

5. Confirm answers.
   (Answers)
   - **Before paraphrasing or summarizing, identify shared language.**
   - **Examples of this are proper nouns, common nouns, dates and figures, and specialized language/terminology.**

6. Then elicit the following:
   - *What is one way to change some shared language?*

7. Confirm answer. (Answer: **Change the word form.**)

Option 3

1. Explain the concept of shared language by writing on the board:
   - *Many people around the world drink tea.*

2. Explain that you will paraphrase this information, then write:
   - *Lots of humans all over the globe enjoy _____ .*

3. Elicit: *What is another way to say "tea"?*

4. Explain:
   - *It is difficult to substitute "tea" for another word with the same or a similar meaning. Therefore, "tea" is shared language.*

Exercise 1

Option 1

1. Have students work individually to complete the exercise.
2. When done, have students compare answers with a partner.
3. Elicit answers.

Option 2

1. Divide the class into pairs or small groups.
2. Have students work collaboratively to complete the exercise.
3. Elicit answers.

Section 2 **Writing paraphrases and summaries**

1. Six steps to writing a paraphrase

Option 1

1. Divide the class into pairs (Student A and Student B).
2. In each pair, have Student A read the six steps, page 78; have Student B keep his or her textbook closed.
3. While Student A is reading, have Student B draw the following table:

Step 1	
Step 2	
Step 3	
Step 4	
Step 5	
Step 6	

4. With books closed, have Student A explain the paraphrasing steps to Student B. Student B should fill in the table.
5. Then have the students compare the information in Student B's table with the information in the textbook.
6. Have all students read the Example on tourism, page 79.

Option 2

1. Have students read the six steps.
2. As students are reading, write "How to paraphrase" on the board, and under it, draw the following table:

Step 1	
Step 2	
Step 3	
Step 4	
Step 5	
Step 6	

3. With books closed, have students in pairs or small groups recall what they read.
4. Then elicit the steps to fill in the table.
5. Have all students read the Example on tourism, page 79.

   Emphasize:
   When paraphrasing:
   - *Change the vocabulary and structure of the original source, but do not change the meaning.*
   - *Do not use more than three words in a row from the original.*
   - *Do not look at the original passage – if you cannot see the original, it will be easier to use your own language to write the paraphrase.*
   - *Although rewording is necessary, it is important not to change the tense of the original sentences, as this will alter the meaning.*

2. Five steps to writing a summary

Option 1

1. Divide the class into pairs (Student A and Student B).
2. Have Student A in each pair read the five steps, pages 79–80; have Student B keep his or her textbook closed.
3. While Student A is reading, have Student B draw the following table:

Step 1	
Step 2	
Step 3	
Step 4	
Step 5	

4. With textbooks closed, have Student A explain the summarizing steps to Student B. Student B should complete the table.

5. Have pairs compare the information in Student B's table with the information in the textbook.

6. Have all students read the Example on the Olympics, pages 80–81.

Option 2

1. Have students read the five steps in the textbook, pages 79–80.

2. As students are reading, write "How to summarize" on the board, and under it, draw the following table:

Step 1	
Step 2	
Step 3	
Step 4	
Step 5	

3. Then, with books closed, have students in pairs or small groups recall what they read.

4. Elicit answers to fill in the table.

5. Have all students read the Example on the Olympics, pages 80–81.

Emphasize:

When summarizing:

- *Change the vocabulary and sentence structure, but do not change the meaning from the original.*
- *Do not use more than three words in a row from the original.*
- *Try not to look at the original passage when writing the summary – too tempting to just copy the words.*
- *The summary should be much shorter than the original.*
- *As with paraphrasing, it is important not to change the tense of the original information so that the meaning stays the same.*

Exercise 2

Option 1

1. Have students work individually to complete the exercise.

2. When done, have students compare answers with a partner.

3. Elicit answers.

Option 2

1. Divide the class into pairs or small groups.

2. Have students work collaboratively to complete the exercise.

3. Elicit answers.

Exercise 3

Option 1

1. Have students work individually to complete the exercise.

2. When done, have students compare answers with a partner.

3. Elicit answers.

Option 2

1. Divide the class into pairs or small groups.

2. Have students work collaboratively to complete the exercise.

3. Elicit answers.

Exercise 4

Option 1

1. Have students work individually to complete the exercise.

2. When done, have students compare answers with a partner.

3. Elicit answers.

Option 2

1. Divide the class into pairs or small groups.

2. Have students work collaboratively to complete the exercise.

3. Elicit answers.

Exercise 5

Do the items one or two at a time and follow any option below. Doing all five items in a row without an answer check may be difficult for students.

Option 1

1. Have students work individually to complete the exercise.

2. When done, have students compare answers with a partner.

3. Elicit answers.

Option 2

1. Divide the class into pairs or small groups.

2. Have students work collaboratively to complete the exercise.

3. Elicit answers.

Option 3

1. Follow steps one and two of Option 2 above.

2. Re-divide students into new pairs or groups so they are sitting with at least one new person.

3. Have them compare answers with each other.

4. Elicit answers.

Exercise 6

Option 1

1. Have students work individually to complete the exercise.

2. When done, have students compare answers with a partner.

3. Elicit answers.

Option 2

1. Divide the class into pairs or small groups.

2. Have students work collaboratively to complete the exercise.

3. Elicit answers.

Exercise 7

Do the items one or two at a time and follow any option below. Doing all three items in a row without an answer check may be difficult for students.

Option 1

1. Have students work individually to complete the exercise.

2. When done, have students compare answers with a partner.

3. Elicit answers.

Option 2

1. Divide the class into pairs or small groups.

2. Have students work collaboratively to complete the exercise.

3. Elicit answers.

Option 3

1. Follow steps one and two of Option 2 above.

2. Re-divide students into new pairs or groups so they are sitting with at least one new person.

3. Have them compare answers with each other.

4. Elicit answers.

Section 3   Using quotations

Option 1

1. Write the following on the board:
   • *When is quoting a source useful?*

2. Have students work in pairs or small groups to discuss the question.

3. Elicit answers and write them on the board.

4. Confirm answer.
   (Answer)
   Consider quoting if:
   • **the source is respected.**
   • **the source is a primary source.**
   • **the words of the original are powerful.**
   • **the original cannot be rewritten effectively.**

5. Then write the following on the board:
   • *Why is using too many quotations a problem?*

6. Have students work in pairs or small groups to discuss the question.

7. Elicit answers and write them on the board.

8. Confirm answer. (Answer: **Too many quotes in an essay make it seem like the whole essay is just someone else's words and ideas.**)

Option 2

1. Have students read the explanations in the textbook, page 85, but stop before the Example.

2. As students are reading, write the following questions on the board:
   • *When is quoting a source useful?*
   • *Why is using too many quotations a problem?*

3. Then, with books closed, have students in pairs or small groups discuss the questions.

4. Elicit answers and write them on the board.

5. Confirm answers.
   (Answers)
   Consider quoting if:
   • **the source is respected.**
   • **the source is a primary source.**
   • **the words of the original are powerful.**
   • **the original cannot be rewritten effectively.**

   Too many quotes in an essay make it seem like the whole essay is just someone else's words and ideas.

Option 3

1. Have students reread the paragraph in the textbook, page 85, which starts with the phrase "How a quotation is introduced . . ."

2. Then have students read the Example on colonization, pages 85–86.

3. As students are reading, write the following questions on the board:
   • *What is the problem with the first body paragraph excerpt?*
   • *Why is the second excerpt better?*

4. Elicit answers.

5. Confirm answers.
   (Answers)
   - **In the first body paragraph excerpt, the quote may be too sudden of a change because it was not what the reader was expecting.**
   - **In the second excerpt, the quote is introduced with an explanation of what the reader can expect. As well, the source itself lends authority.**
6. Emphasize:
   - *A quotation should be properly introduced to maintain cohesion in the essay. Prepare readers for the quote.*

Option 4

1. Follow Option 3 above.
2. Then write the following on the board:
   - *One way to ensure the well-being of the country's population is to teach children how to manage their money. "Almost half of all Americans reach retirement age without any money saved" (American Society of Retirees).*
   - *What is wrong with this?*
3. Have students work in pairs or small groups to discuss the question.
4. Elicit answers and write them on the board.
5. Confirm answer.
   (Answer)
   - **The quote is not introduced properly. The reader might be expecting information on ways to teach children about managing money.**
   - **The quote should be introduced explaining that there is a consequence to a lack of education about money.**
6. Have students work in pairs or small groups to discuss this question:
   - *How can the quotation be introduced to maintain better cohesion?*
7. Elicit answers and write them on the board.
8. (Example answer)
   One way to ensure the well-being of the country's population is to teach children how to manage their money. It is apparent that such education is necessary, based on information from an American Society of Retirees report: "Almost half of all Americans reach retirement age without any money saved."

   Emphasize:
   - *Avoid using too many quotes because it makes the essay rely too heavily on other people's words and ideas.*
   - *Quoting should only be used when the exact wording has a high degree of impact on the reader.*
   - *Sometimes the exact words from the original source can be confusing, so paraphrasing or summarizing can make it easier for the reader to understand the source information.*

Integrating quotations

Option 1

1. Have students read the explanation in the textbook, pages 86–88.
2. As students are reading, draw the following table on the board:

	Introduced with . . .	*Punctuation*	*Capitalization*
Way 1			
Way 2			
Way 3			
Way 4			
Way 5			

3. Then, with books closed, have students in pairs or small groups recall what they read.
4. Elicit answers to fill in the table.
5. Have students open their book to pages 86–88 and check that what is written on the board is accurate.
6. Confirm answers.
   (Answers)
   Way 1
   Introduced with . . .: Phrase
   Punctuation: Comma after phrase; quotation marks
   Capitalization: Yes

   Way 2
   Introduced with . . .: Complete sentence
   Punctuation: Colon after phrase; quotation marks
   Capitalization: Yes

   Way 3
   Introduced with . . .: Phrase using "that"
   Punctuation: None after "that"; quotation marks
   Capitalization: No

   Way 4
   Introduced with . . .: Phrase embedded in quote
   Punctuation: Commas before and after intro phrase
   Capitalization: Yes

   Way 5
   Introduced with . . .: Sentence or phrase
   Punctuation: Colon after intro phrase, no quotation marks, indentation
   Capitalization: Yes

Option 2

1. Have students read the first two ways to integrate a quotation, pages 86–87.

2. As students are reading, write the following questions on the board:
   - *How are the two ways different and similar?*

3. Then, with books closed, have students work in pairs or small groups to discuss the question.

4. Elicit answers and write them on the board.

5. Have students open their book to pages 86–87 and check that what is written on the board is accurate.

6. Confirm answers.
   (Answers)
   - **1st way – introduced with a phrase followed by a comma**
   - **2nd way – introduced with a complete sentence followed by a colon**
   - **Both ways – quote begins with a capital letter**

7. Then have students read the next two ways to integrate a quotation, page 87.

8. With books closed, have students work in pairs or small groups to discuss the question again.

9. Elicit answers and write them on the board.

10. Have students open their book to page 87 and check that what is written on the board is accurate.

11. Confirm answers.
    (Answers)
    - **3rd way – no comma necessary if blended using the word "that," and quote begins with a small letter**
    - **4th way – introductory phrase is inside the quote, separated from the quote by commas**
    - **no similarity**

12. Then have students read the fifth way to integrate a quotation, page 88.

13. As students are reading, write the following question on the board:
    - *How is this way different from the other ways?*

14. Then, with books closed, have students work in pairs or small groups to discuss the question again.

15. Elicit answers and write them on the board.

16. Have students open their book to page 88 and check that what is written on the board is accurate.

17. Confirm answer.
    (Answer)
    - **5th way – no quotation marks necessary, start quote on a separate line, whole quote should be indented, restart rest of paragraph on a separate line**

    Emphasize:
    - *Try to use a variety of quotation techniques to keep the essay style interesting and engaging for the reader.*

Option 1

1. Have students work individually to complete the exercise.

2. When done, have students compare answers with a partner.

3. Elicit answers.

Option 2

1. Divide the class into pairs or small groups.

2. Have students work collaboratively to complete the exercise.

3. Elicit answers.

Section 1	Citation components and integration

Option 1

1. Write the following on the board:
   - *What is citation?*
   - *Why is it included in an essay?*

2. Have students work in pairs or small groups to discuss the questions.

3. Elicit answers and write them on the board.

4. Confirm answers.
   (Answers)
   Citation is identifying the source of information. It is included in an essay to:
   - **avoid plagiarism by identifying the actual source of information.**
   - **establish the credibility of the essay by identifying the credible sources.**
   - **enable readers to find the original source.**

Option 2

1. Have students read the explanation on page 89, but stop before "1. References."

2. As students are reading, write the following questions on the board:
   - *What is citation?*
   - *Why is it included in an essay?*
   - *What are the two components of citation?*

3. Then, with books closed, have students work in pairs or small groups to discuss the questions.

4. Elicit answers and write them on the board.

5. Confirm answers.
   (Answers)
   Citation is identifying the source of information. It is included in an essay to:
   - **avoid plagiarism by identifying the actual source of information.**
   - **establish the credibility of the essay by identifying the credible sources.**
   - **enable readers to find the original source.**

   The two components are a References list and in-text citation.

   Emphasize:
   - *These two elements of citation work together–in-text citation refers to the References list. The principle is that in-text citation gives basic information (author name and year of publication), and the References list can be used if readers want to check this information for themselves.*

1. References

Option 1

1. Write the following on the board:
   - *Why is a References list necessary?*

2. Have students work in pairs or small groups to discuss the question.

3. Elicit answers and write them on the board.

4. Confirm answer.
   (Answer)
   A References list is necessary to show:
   - **that the essay was well researched.**
   - **where exactly readers can find certain information cited in the essay.**

Option 2

1. Have students look at the sample References list for the model essay on Antarctica on pages 58–59.

2. As students are reading, write the following questions on the board:
   - *In what order are the reference entries presented?*
   - *If there is an author(s), how is the author's name presented?*
   - *Why do some entries not have an author?*
   - *Why do some parentheses have only the year and other ones have the year and then other information?*
   - *For a website URL, what phrase do you put before it?*

3. Have students work in pairs or small groups to discuss the questions using the References list.

4. Elicit answers and write them on the board.

5. Confirm answers.
   (Answers)
   - **The reference entries are in alphabetical order.**
   - **The author's name is presented last name first, then first initial. (For two authors, separate with "&" and present names in order as they appeared in the original.)**
   - **Some entries do not have an author because there was no author listed in the original.**
   - **Entries for academic journals only have the year. If there is a year and actual month and date, then it likely came from a source published periodically, such as the online version of a magazine or website.**
   - **The phrase to put before a URL is "Retrieved from."**

   Emphasize:
   - *Although making a References list seems like an overwhelming task, there are several online programs that will automatically format a reference entry just by cutting and pasting the URL.*

2. In-text citation

Option 1

1. Have students read the information under Pattern 1.

2. As students are reading, write the following on the board:
   What does this pattern emphasize?

3. Elicit answers and write them on the board.

4. Confirm answers.
   (Answer)
   Pattern 1: See bullet points on textbook page 90.

5. Follow the same procedure for Pattern 2 and then Pattern 3.
   (Answers)
   Pattern 2: See bullet points on textbook page 90.

   Pattern 3: See bullet points on textbook page 91.

Option 2

1. Have students read the explanation and examples of the three patterns on pages 90–91.

2. As students are reading, write the following on the board:
   • *What information should be included in the text to tell readers where particular sourced information came from?*
   • *Why does this information help the reader?*

3. Have students work in pairs or small groups to discuss the questions.

4. Elicit answers and write them on the board.

5. Confirm answers.
   (Answers)
   In-text citation should include:
   • **The information on the particular source which appears first in its entry on the References list – helps readers find the entry easily on the References list, which is in alphabetical order.**
   • **The year – in case several pieces of information came from the same source, the year [+ month/date] tells readers which particular entry is the source of particular information.**

   Emphasize:
   • *The in-text citation should tell readers which sourced information belongs to which entry on the References list.*

Option 3

1. Have students read the explanations for the three patterns of in-text citation integration, pages 90–91.

2. As students are reading, draw the following table on the board:

	Order	Example
Pattern 1		
Pattern 2		
Pattern 3		

3. Then, with books closed, have students in pairs or small groups recall the three patterns.

4. Elicit answers to fill in the middle column of the table.

5. Have students open their book to pages 90–91 and check that what is written on the board is accurate.

6. Then again, with books closed, have students in pairs or small groups recall the example given in the textbook for each of the three patterns.

7. Elicit answers to fill in the right column of the table.

   NOTE: Students do not have to remember the exact wording of the examples, just the general information plus the source and year, in the proper order according to the pattern.

8. Have students open their book to pages 90–91 and check that what is written on the board is accurate.

9. Confirm answers.

   Emphasize:
   • *Consider the effect you would like a sentence to have on the reader, then choose the appropriate citation pattern.*
   • *If possible, use a variety of patterns to keep the essay style interesting for the reader.*

Option 4

1. Draw the following table on the board:

	Order	Example
Pattern 1		
Pattern 2		
Pattern 3		

2. Divide the class into groups of three and have each group draw the table as above.

3. Then have each student in each group read a different pattern in the textbook, pages 90–91.

4. When done, have students close their textbook and work collaboratively to fill in the middle and right columns of the table.

5. Have students open their book to pages 90–91 and check their answers.

Option 5

1. Follow Option 3 or 4 above.
2. Then, below the table on the board, write the following:
   - *There is a need to establish firm rules, as previous agreements are apparently inadequate to protect Antarctica's eco-system.*
3. Then:
   - have students look at the References list for the Antarctica essay on pages 58–59.
   - inform them that the information below the table on the board is from the second to last entry on the References list (starts with "Tourists . . .").
   - have students write a complete sentence of an in-text citation for each pattern on the board.
4. Have students open their book to pages 90–91 and check their answers.
5. Elicit answers and write them on the board.
6. Confirm answers.
   (Example answers)
   - **Pattern 1:**
     There is a need to establish firm rules, as previous agreements are apparently inadequate to protect Antarctica's eco-system (Tourists, 2009, December 21).
   - **Pattern 2:**
     The article "Tourists in Antarctica cause of major concern" (2009) emphasizes that there is a need to establish firm rules, as previous agreements are apparently inadequate to protect Antarctica's eco-system.
   - **Pattern 3:**
     In a 2009 *ScienceDaily* article, there is a need to establish firm rules, as previous agreements are apparently inadequate to protect Antarctica's eco-system (Tourists).

   Emphasize:
   - *When the source entry is the title of an article, the whole title is not necessary if the source is in parentheses – you need just enough words from the title to help readers find the information in the References list.*

Exercise 1

Option 1

1. Have students work individually to complete the exercise.
2. When done, have students compare answers with a partner.
3. Elicit answers.

Option 2

1. Divide the class into pairs or small groups.
2. Have students work collaboratively to complete the exercise.
3. Elicit answers.

Option 3

1. Follow steps one and two of Option 2 above.
2. Re-divide students into new pairs or groups so they are sitting with at least one new person.
3. Have them compare answers with each other.
4. Elicit answers.

Section 2 Common knowledge

Option 1

1. Write the following question on the board:
   - *Does every fact in an essay always need to be cited?*
2. Have students work in pairs or small groups to discuss the question.
3. Elicit answers and write them on the board.
4. Confirm answer. (Answer: **No, if the information is considered common knowledge**)
5. Then write the following question on the board:
   - *What is common knowledge?*
6. Have students work in pairs or small groups to discuss the question.
7. Elicit answers and write them on the board. (Students are likely to incorrectly answer "Something that most people know.")
8. Test the validity of this answer by asking:
   - *How many times has England won the FIFA World Cup?* (Answer: **Once, in 1966**)
   - *What is the capital of Zimbabwe?* (Answer: **Harare**)
   - *Are these pieces of information considered common knowledge?* (The students are likely to incorrectly answer "No, because many people in the class did not know them.")

   Emphasize:
   - *They are considered common knowledge as they are established facts. Their accuracy can be confirmed from a variety of sources.*

Option 2

1. Have students read the explanation on page 92.
2. Test students' understanding of the idea of "common knowledge" by writing on the board:
   - *As a teenager in Germany, Pope Benedict XVI was a member of the German army, helping with antiaircraft guns.*
   - *The speed of sound varies at different altitudes.*
3. Then ask: *Do these sentences require citation?*
4. Have students work in pairs or small groups to discuss the question.

5. Elicit and confirm answer. (Answer: **These sentences do not have to be cited because they are considered common knowledge, as they are facts. The first is a historical fact, the second a scientific one.**)

Emphasize:

- *If the writer is not sure whether or not the information is considered common knowledge, it is better to include citation.*

Exercise 2

Option 1

1. Have students work individually to complete the exercise.
2. When done, have students compare answers with a partner.
3. Elicit answers.

Option 2

1. Divide the class into pairs or small groups.
2. Have students work collaboratively to complete the exercise.
3. Elicit answers.

UNIT 3

Part 4
Using reporting verbs and phrases

To introduce the idea of variations in reporting verbs:

1. Write the following question on the board:
   - *"Says" is probably the most common reporting verb. What are some other reporting verbs?*

2. Have students work in pairs or small groups to brainstorm answers to the question.

3. Elicit answers and write them on the board.

4. Then elicit:
   - *Do all of these reporting verbs have the same meaning?*

5. Confirm answer. (Answer: **No, certain reporting verbs are more appropriate than others depending on the information being reported and the source's position on the information.**)

Section 1 — Using reporting verbs

Option 1

1. Have students go one pattern at a time and:
   - read the explanation on pages 94–96.
   - do the accompanying exercise (Exercises 1, 2, and 3).

   NOTE: When doing the exercise, have students work in pairs or small groups.

2. Check answers after each exercise, but elicit the pattern first and write it on the board.

Option 2

1. Draw the following table on the board:

	Order	Example
Pattern 1		
Pattern 2		
Pattern 3		

2. Divide the class into groups of three and have each group draw the table as above.

3. Then have each student in each group read a different pattern in the textbook, pages 94–96.

4. When done, have students close their textbook and work collaboratively to complete the middle column of the table.

5. Have students open their book to pages 94–96 and check their answers.

6. Elicit answers and fill in the table on the board.

7. Then, again with books closed:
   - have students in pairs or small groups try to recall the example given in the textbook for each of the three patterns.
   - write the example in the right column of the table.

   NOTE: Students do not have to remember the exact wording of the examples, just the general information plus the source and year, in the correct order according to the pattern.

8. Have students open their book to pages 94–96 and check their answers.

9. Elicit answers and fill in the table on the board.

Exercises 1, 2, and 3

Option 1

1. Have students work individually to complete the exercise.

2. When done, have students compare answers with a partner.

3. Elicit answers.

Option 2

1. Divide the class into pairs or small groups.

2. Have students work collaboratively to complete the exercise.

3. Elicit answers.

Pattern variations

Option 1

1. Draw the following table on the board:

	Order	Example
Variation A		
Variation B		
Variation C		
Variation D		

2. Divide the class into pairs or small groups and draw the table as above.

3. Have students go one pattern at a time and read the explanation and examples on page 97.

4. Then, with books closed, have students try to recall the pattern and the examples.

   NOTE: Students do not have to remember the exact wording of the examples, just the general information plus the source and year, in the correct order according to the pattern.

5. Elicit pattern and examples and fill in the table.

Option 2

1. Draw the following table on the board:

	Order	Example
Variation A		
Variation B		
Variation C		
Variation D		

2. Divide the class into pairs or groups of four students.

3. Have each pair/group draw the table as above.

4. Then have each student in each pair read two pattern variations, or each student in each group of four read one different pattern on page 97.

5. When done, have students close their textbook and work collaboratively to complete the middle and right columns of the table by recalling their particular pattern and examples.

   NOTE: Students do not have to remember the exact wording of the examples, just the general information plus the source and year, in the correct order according to the pattern.

6. Have students open their book to page 97 and check their answers.

7. Elicit answers and fill in the table on the board.

Option 3

1. Write the following on the board:
   • *(source) World Poverty Foundation, 2012*
   • *(information) Education is the most effective way to fight poverty.*

2. Have students individually, in pairs, or in small groups write as many sentences as possible using different patterns and reporting verbs.

3. Select students to come to the board and write one of their sentences.

4. Check for accuracy.

   Emphasize:
   • *Try to use a variety of different patterns in order to keep the essay style interesting for the reader.*

Meaning and strength of reporting verbs

Option 1

1. Write the following on the board:
   • *Professor Evan Schmidt (2012) of the University of Springfield says that traditional Freudian psychotherapy is ineffective.*
   • *Professor Evan Schmidt (2012) of the University of Springfield implies that traditional Freudian psychotherapy is ineffective.*
   • *Professor Evan Schmidt (2012) of the University of Springfield concluded that traditional Freudian psychotherapy is ineffective.*
   • *Professor Evan Schmidt (2012) of the University of Springfield criticizes traditional Freudian psychotherapy for being ineffective.*

2. Then ask: *Do all of these sentences have the same meaning?*

3. Have students work in pairs or small groups to discuss the question.

4. Elicit and confirm answers.
   (Answer)
   No.
   • **Sentence 1 – rather neutral**
   • **Sentence 2 – not directly stated**
   • **Sentence 3 – likely makes claim as a result of research**
   • **Sentence 4 – critical attitude regarding subject**

Option 2

1. Have students read the explanation and examples in the textbook, page 98.

2. As students are reading, write the following questions on the board:
   • *What are two things you need to consider when choosing a reporting verb?*
   • *What is the problem with neutral reporting verbs?*

3. Then, with books closed, have students in pairs or small groups answer the two questions.

4. Elicit answers and write them on the board.

5. Confirm answers.
   (Answers)
   • **First question – 1) the meaning of the source information, and 2) the strength of the author's attitude toward the information**
   • **Second question – 1) They may not accurately convey the meaning of the source information or the strength of the author's position, and 2) particular neutral reporting verbs are often overused**

Option 1

1. Have students work individually to complete the exercise.
2. When done, have students compare answers with a partner.
3. Elicit answers.

Option 2

1. Divide the class into pairs or small groups.
2. Have students work collaboratively to complete the exercise.
3. Elicit answers.

UNIT 4
Part 1
Hedging and intensifying

Section 1 — Using hedging and intensifying

Option 1

1. Write the following on the board:
   - *People move away from the countryside and into big cities for a more exciting life.*
   - *How accurate is this statement?*

2. Have students work in pairs or small groups to discuss the question.

3. Elicit answers and write them on the board.

4. Confirm answer. (Answer: **It is not entirely accurate as too many sweeping generalizations are made – 100% of people? Only for a more exciting life?**)

5. Then ask: *How can this statement be fixed?*

6. Have students work in pairs or small groups to discuss the question and write at least two possible alternative sentences.

7. Elicit answers and write them on the board.

8. Give possible answers.
   (Possible answers)
   - **Many people move away from the countryside and into big cities for a more exciting life.**
   - **People move away from the countryside and into big cities mainly for a more exciting life.**

Option 2

1. Have students read the explanations in the textbook, pages 102–103.

2. As students are reading, write the following questions on the board:
   - *What is hedging? What were some examples given?*
   - *What is intensifying? What were some examples given?*

3. Then, with books closed, have students in pairs or small groups discuss the questions.

4. Elicit answers and write them on the board.

5. Confirm answers.
   (Answers)
   - **Hedging – using words to reduce the certainty of statements**
   - **Intensifying – using words to increase the certainty of statements**
   - **Examples of both – see textbook, pages 102–103**

Section 2 — Vocabulary for hedging and intensifying

1. Divide the class into pairs.

2. Draw the following table on the board:

Hedging		Intensifying
	Verbs	
	Modal verbs	
	Adjectives	
	Adverbs	

3. Have student pairs draw the same table.

4. Then, with the table on page 104:
   - have one student of each pair memorize the words under "Hedging."
   - have the other student memorize the words under "Intensifying."

   Give them no more than one or two minutes.

5. With books closed, have students teach each other the words they memorized and fill in the table.

6. Elicit answers and fill in the table on the board.

7. Emphasize:
   - *Many of the words in the table can be paired to modify them further.*

8. Have students read the examples on page 104.

Exercises 1, 2, 3, and 4

Option 1

1. Have students work individually to complete the exercise.

2. When done, have students compare answers with a partner.

3. Elicit answers.

Option 2

1. Divide the class into pairs or small groups.

2. Have students work collaboratively to complete the exercise.

3. Elicit answers.

UNIT 4

Part 2
Academic sentence styles

Section 1 **Conjunctions**

1. Coordinating conjunctions

Option 1

1. Write the following on the board:
   - *Professor Nate Nakamura researched ways to clone farm animals. He finally developed ways to do this. He cloned sheep. He also cloned chickens. Dr. Nakamura has been the target of protests by various religious groups. Animal rights groups have also targeted him. These groups question the ethics behind such science.*
   - *What is wrong with these sentences?*

2. Have students work in pairs or small groups to discuss the question.

3. Elicit answers and write them on the board.

4. Confirm answers.
   (Possible answers)
   - **The sentences are too short, showing poor academic style.**
   - **They need conjunctions.**

5. With books closed, have students in pairs or small groups try to combine all of these ideas into one sentence.

6. Select certain students to come up to the board and write their sentence.

7. Check grammar and style.

8. Have students open their book to page 108 and check the "Nate Nakamura" example.

Option 2

1. Have students read the explanation and examples in the textbook, pages 108–109.

2. As students are reading, write the following questions on the board:
   - *What are some examples of coordinating conjunctions?*
   - *What were some of the example sentences given?*
   - *What was mentioned about commas?*

3. With books closed, have students in pairs or small groups discuss the questions.

4. Have students open their book to pages 108–109 and check their answers.

5. Elicit and confirm answers.
   (Answers)
   - **Examples –** *for, and, nor, but, or,* etc.
   - **Example sentences – See textbook pages 108–109.**
   - **Comma – used before coordinating conjunction followed by a full clause, used as a serial comma to more clearly separate two items**

   Emphasize:
   - *Frequent use of coordinating conjunctions is an essential part of academic writing style because it allows the writer to concisely express a lot of information in a single sentence.*

2. Correlative conjunctions

Option 1

1. Write the following on the board:
   - *Ruth Mark was in jail for 15 years for her political beliefs, and while jailed, she continued to be actively involved in the democratic movement.*
   - *This sentence sounds flat. How can it be improved?*

2. Have students work in pairs or small groups to discuss the question and write a new sentence.

3. Select certain students to come up to the board and write their sentence.

4. Give possible answer.
   (Possible answer)
   Not only was Ruth Mark in jail for 15 years for her political beliefs, but also while jailed, she continued to be actively involved in the democratic movement.

   The revised sentence emphasizes the achievement of both points.

Option 2

1. Have students read the explanation and examples in the textbook, page 109.

2. As students are reading, write the following questions on the board:
   - *What are some examples of correlative conjunctions?*
   - *What was the example sentence given?*

3. With books closed, have students work in pairs or small groups to discuss the questions.

4. Have students open their book to page 109 and check the answers.

5. Elicit and confirm answers.
(Answers)
- **Examples – *both . . . and, not only . . . but also, either . . . or,* etc.**
- **Example sentence – See textbook page 109.**

Emphasize:
- *Correlative conjunctions are useful for emphasizing the relationship between ideas.*

3. Subordinating conjunctions

Option 1

1. Write the following on the board:
   - *Many heads of terrorist groups have been killed or captured in the past year, but suicide attacks have actually increased over the same period.*
   - *This sentence sounds flat. How can it be improved?*

2. Have students work in pairs or small groups to discuss the question and write a new sentence.

3. Have students open their book to pages 109–110 and check the answer.

4. Elicit and confirm answer. (Answer: **See textbook, page 110, example sentence next to "Showing opposition and contrast."**)

5. Elicit: What does "subordinate" mean?

6. Confirm answer.
(Example answer)
- **A subordinate is one thing which depends on another.**
- **So a subordinating conjunction shows how one part of a sentence depends on, or is subordinate to, a more important part of the sentence.**

Option 2

1. Have students read the explanation and examples in the textbook, pages 109–110.

2. As students are reading, write the following questions on the board:
   - *What are some examples of subordinating conjunctions?*
   - *What were some of the example sentences given?*
   - *What was mentioned about commas?*

3. With books closed, have students in pairs or small groups discuss the questions.

4. Have students open their book to pages 109–110 and check the answers.

5. Elicit and confirm answers.
(Answers)
- **Examples – See table, page 110.**
- **Example sentences – See textbook, page 110.**
- **Comma – used between the clauses if the dependent clause comes first**

Option 3

1. Divide the class into pairs.

2. Draw the following table on the board:

	Words	Example sentences
Showing opposition and contrast		
Introducing an alternative		
Showing chronological order or a sequence		
Showing cause and effect		

3. Have student pairs draw the same table.

4. Then have students look at the table in the textbook, page 110, and:
   - have one student in each pair memorize the words and example sentences in the top two categories of the table.
   - have the other student memorize the words and example sentences in the other two categories.
   Give them no more than one or two minutes.

5. Then, with books closed, have students teach each other the words and sentences they memorized and fill in the table.

6. Elicit answers and fill in the table on the board.

4. Subjunctive adverbs

Option 1

1. Write the following on the board:
   - *Police work often requires strenuous physical activity. Entry requirements for many police forces include physical health and fitness criteria.*
   - *How can these two sentences be linked while keeping them as separate sentences?*

2. Have students work in pairs or small groups to discuss the question and write a new sentence.

3. Elicit possible answers.

4. Have students open their books to check the answer. (Answer: **See textbook, page 111, first example sentence in the table.**)

Option 2

1. Have students read the explanation and examples in the textbook.

2. As students are reading, write the following questions on the board:
   - *What are some examples of subjunctive adverbs?*
   - *What were some of the example sentences given?*
   - *What was mentioned about commas?*

3. With books closed, have students in pairs or small groups discuss the questions.

4. Have students open their book to pages 111–112 and check the answers.

5. Elicit and confirm answers.
   (Answers)
   - **Examples – See table in textbook, page 111.**
   - **Example sentences – See textbook, page 111.**
   - **Comma – necessary**

   Emphasize:
   - *Students should attempt to use all three different positions of subjunctive adverbs in their essays to ensure variety in their writing style.*

Option 3

1. Divide the class into groups of three.

2. Draw the following table on the board:

The idea is a logical conclusion from the previous idea
Examples:
Example sentences:
The idea contrasts with the previous idea
Examples:
Example sentences:
The idea supports the previous idea
Examples:
Example sentences:

3. Have the student groups draw the same table.

4. Then have students look at the table in the textbook, page 111, and:
   - have each group member memorize a different category of words and example sentences.
   - then, with books closed, have students teach each other the words and sentences they memorized and fill in the table.

5. Elicit answers and fill in the table on the board.

Section 2 Linking ideas with punctuation

Option 1

1. Write the following on the board:
   - *The North American black bear population remains strong, but the Asian black bear population is decreasing.*
   - *In most countries around the world, people routinely and legally use three of the most addictive drugs, which are alcohol, nicotine, and caffeine.*
   - *In which sentence can a colon be used? And in which sentence can a semi-colon be used?*

2. With books closed, have students work in pairs or small groups to discuss the questions.

3. Have students open their book to page 112 and check their answers.

Option 2

1. Have students read the explanation and examples in the textbook.

2. As students are reading, write the following on the board:
   - *When is a colon useful?*
   - *When is a semi-colon useful?*
   - *What are some of the example sentences where they are used?*

3. Then, with books closed, have students work in pairs or small groups to discuss the questions and recall the example sentences.

4. Have students open their book to pages 112–113 to check their answers.

5. Confirm answers.
   (Answers)
   - **Colon – indicates an explanation or example is following**
   - **Semi-colon – can replace conjunctions; shows the close relationship between two ideas**
   - **Example sentences – See textbook, pages 112–113.**

   Emphasize:
   - *Colons and semi-colons are rarely used in student essays, but they are an effective way of adding variety to the essay style.*
   - *Both the semi-colon and colon show the close relationship between information.*

Exercise 1

Do the items one or two at a time and follow any option below. Doing all of the items in a row without an answer check may be difficult for students.

NOTE: The usefulness of this exercise depends on how much students attempt to use vocabulary or structures they are unfamiliar with, so encourage students to use "new" words.

Option 1

1. Have students work individually to complete the exercise.
2. When done, have students compare answers with a partner.
3. Elicit answers.

Option 2

1. Divide the class into pairs or small groups.
2. Have students work collaboratively to complete the exercise.
3. Elicit answers.

Option 3

1. Follow steps one and two of Option 2 above.
2. Re-divide students into new pairs or groups so they are sitting with at least one new person.
3. Have them compare answers with each other.
4. Elicit answers.

Section 3 Sentences in context

Option 1

1. Have students read the explanation and examples in the textbook, page 115.
2. As students are reading, write the following on the board:
   - *Why is B better than A?*
   - *Why is D better than C?*
3. Then have students look at examples A and B and explain to each other in their own words the answer to the first question.
4. Elicit answers.
5. Then have students look at examples C and D and explain to each other in their own words the answer to the second question.
6. Elicit answers.

Option 2

1. Divide class into pairs.
2. Have students open their textbook to page 115 and:
   - have one student in each pair read the explanation and examples for sentences A and B.
   - have the other student read the explanation and examples for sentences C and D.
3. As students are reading, write the following on the board:
   - *Why is B better than A?*
   - *Why is D better than C?*
4. Then have students explain to each other in words different than the textbook the answer to the two questions.
5. Elicit answers.

Option 3

1. From the textbook, page 115, write examples A and B on the board.
2. Have students work in pairs or small groups to discuss: Which sentence is better?
3. Write examples C and D on the board.
4. Have students work in pairs or small groups to discuss: Which sentence is better?
5. Have students read the explanation in the textbook, page 115, to check their answers.

   Emphasize:
   - *In general, information is easier to understand when one sentence begins with information or ideas that have been introduced in a previous sentence. For example, compare:*
     - *Neil Armstrong was the first person to walk on the moon. He achieved this in1969.*
     - *Neil Armstrong was the first person to walk on the moon. 1969 was the year in which he achieved this.*

   In the first example, the second sentence begins with a subject that has already been introduced in the previous sentence, and is therefore easier for the reader to follow.

   - *This is the "standard" writing pattern in English. While breaking this pattern can be an effective technique for emphasis, the majority of sentences should follow this pattern so the essay is easy to read.*

Exercise 2

Do the items one or two at a time and follow any option below. Doing all of the items in a row without an answer check may be difficult for students.

Option 1

1. Have students work individually to complete the exercise.
2. When done, have students compare answers with a partner.
3. Elicit answers.

Option 2

1. Divide the class into pairs or small groups.
2. Have students work collaboratively to complete the exercise.
3. Elicit answers.

Section 4 — Active, passive, and nominalization

Option 1

1. Write the following on the board:
   - *Many people around the world speak English.*
   - *English is spoken around the world.*
   - *Some people attend a famous university to get status.*
   - *Attending a famous university is a way to get status for some people.*
   - *Which sentence is an example of active, passive, and nominalization?*

2. Then, with books closed, have students work in pairs or groups to discuss the question.

3. Elicit and confirm answer.
   (Answer)
   - **Active – sentences 1 and 3**
   - **Passive – sentence 2**
   - **Nominalization – sentence 4**

4. Emphasize:
   - *The passive form and nominalization are used often in academic writing to emphasize something other than the agent – the "doer" of the action.*

Option 2

1. Have students read the explanation and examples in the textbook, pages 117–118, under "1. Passive sentences."

2. As students are reading, write the following on the board:
   - *When are passive sentences useful?*
   - *What were some examples of passive sentences in the textbook?*
   - *When are nominalizations useful?*
   - *What were some examples of sentences with nominalization in the textbook?*

3. Then, with books closed, have students work in pairs or small groups to discuss the first two questions and recall the example sentences.

4. Then have students open their book to pages 117–118 and check their answers.

5. Confirm answers and examples. (Answers: **See textbook, pages 117–118.**)

6. Then have students read the explanation and examples in the textbook, page 118, under "2. Nominalizations."

7. With books closed, have students work in pairs or small groups to discuss the last two questions and recall the example sentences.

8. Then have students open their book to page 118 and check their answers.

9. Confirm answers and examples. (Answers: **See textbook, page 118.**)

   Emphasize:
   - *Passive and nominalization are more common in academic English than spoken English because they help to imply objectivity, and because they help to express ideas concisely.*

- *All three of these styles should be used in an essay because it makes the writing style more interesting.*
- *It is important to understand the reasons for using these three styles in order to present information and ideas in a "natural" way.*

Exercises 3 and 4

Do the items two or three at a time and follow any option below. Doing all of the items in a row without an answer check may be difficult for students.

NOTE: Exercise 3 may be difficult, so remind students to carefully refer to the previous explanations about the uses of active, passive, and nominalization.

Option 1

1. Have students work individually to complete the exercise.

2. When done, have students compare answers with a partner.

3. Elicit answers.

Option 2

1. Divide the class into pairs or small groups.

2. Have students work collaboratively to complete the exercise.

3. Elicit answers.

UNIT 4

Part 3
Editing

To introduce the idea of editing:
1. Write the following questions on the board:
   - *Why is editing important?*
   - *What should you look for when editing?*
   - *How many times should you edit your essay?*
2. Have students work in pairs or small groups to discuss the questions.
3. Elicit answers and write them on the board.
4. Confirm answers.
   (Answers)
   - **Editing helps improve an essay so that it is more effective, academic, and easy to understand for the reader.**
   - **Therefore, writers should look for errors in grammar and wording as well as ways to improve style and effectiveness.**
   - **Edit it as many times as necessary to where an outside reader has no difficulty understanding it and does not spot any mistakes.**

Emphasize:
- *Readers and especially evaluators of essays get annoyed by two things:*
  - *an essay that is difficult to understand.*
  - *an essay that is filled with mistakes.*
- *Many students are in a rush to submit any draft because they procrastinate. But submitting an inadequately edited essay draft is perhaps worse than submitting a properly edited draft late.*
- *The quality of ideas and information in an essay will not be appreciated if these things are not well presented. Editing is a way to ensure that the reader will appreciate the quality of the writer's ideas.*

Section 1 Checking effectiveness

Option 1

To review points taught in the textbook:
1. Write the following question on the board:
   - *What does an effective introductory paragraph have?*
2. Have students work in pairs or small groups to discuss the questions.
3. Elicit answers and write them on the board.
4. Have students open their book to page 122 and check the editing questions under "1. Introductory paragraph."
5. Review the points under each question.
6. Then write the following question on the board:
   - *What do effective body paragraphs have?*

7. Have students work in pairs or small groups to discuss the question.
8. Elicit answers and write them on the board.
9. Have students open their book to pages 123–124 and check the questions under "2. Body paragraphs."
10. Review the points under each question.

    NOTE: Question 4 on page 124 is more relevant to argumentative essays than other essay genres. If writing an essay on a controversial topic which people do not agree on, try to include opposing arguments (counter-arguments) and show why these are not correct (rebuttals).
11. Then write the following question on the board:
    - *What does an effective concluding paragraph have?*
12. Have students work in pairs or small groups to discuss the question.
13. Elicit answers and write them on the board.
14. Have students open their book to page 124 and check the questions under "3. Concluding paragraph."
15. Review the points under each question.

Option 2

1. Have students look at question 2 under "2. Body paragraphs" on page 123.
2. Demonstrate the technique for checking topic sentences by using the model essay on nuclear energy in Unit 1 (page 24) or the model essay on Antarctica in Unit 2 (page 53).

   Emphasize:
   - *After doing this technique, the thesis should combine with the topic sentences to be one coherent and logical paragraph. If it does not, then change the language of the topic sentences.*

Section 2 Checking mechanics

1. Language

Review points taught in the textbook.
1. Write the following question on the board:
   - *What do you remember about hedging and intensifying language?*
2. Have students work in pairs or small groups to discuss the question.
3. Elicit answers and write them on the board.
4. Have students open their book to page 124.
5. Review the goals under questions 2 and 3.

6. Also, re-emphasize selected points from pages 102–104.

7. Then write the following question on the board:
   - *What do you remember about how to create cohesion between information?*

8. Have students work in pairs or small groups to discuss the question.

9. Elicit answers and write them on the board.

10. Confirm answer. (Answer: **Use transitional words and phrases.**)

11. Then review transitional words and phrases by asking:
    - *What transitional words/phrases do you remember?*

12. Have students work in pairs or small groups to brainstorm answers to the question.

13. Elicit answers and write them on the board.

14. Re-emphasize selected points from pages 108–111.

15. Then write the following question on the board:
    - *What do you remember about the passive form and nominalization?*

16. Have students work in pairs or small groups to discuss the question.

17. Elicit answers and write them on the board.

18. Have students open their book to page 125.

19. Review the goal under question 5.

20. Re-emphasize:
    - *Many times, the agent or "doer" of an action is less important than the action itself or the result of it, which is why the passive form and nominalization are used often in academic essays.*

21. Also, re-emphasize selected points from pages 117–118.

22. Have students read question 6 and the point and examples under it, page 125.

23. As students are reading, write the following questions on the board:
    - *What is redundancy?*
    - *What examples were given in the book?*

24. With books closed, have students in pairs or small groups discuss the questions.

25. Elicit answers and write them on the board.

26. Confirm answers.
    (Answers)
    - **Redundancy – words and sentences which are unnecessarily repeated**
    - **Examples – See textbook, page 125.**

27. Emphasize:
    - *A variety of words should be used in an essay. Repetition of words is poor style.*
    - *Repeating sentences should be avoided. An essay should be the building of an idea, not a repetition of one.*

28. Have students read question 7 and the point under it, page 125.

29. As students are reading, write the following question on the board:
    - *What language should you avoid?*

30. Elicit answers and write them on the board.

31. Confirm answer. (Answer: **First- and second-person pronouns – *I, we, us, you***)

    NOTE: This aspect of academic writing is only mentioned briefly because it is assumed that students at this level are familiar with these ideas. However, it is essential to avoid these mistakes because a few small mistakes regarding any of these points will have a big effect on the tone of the essay.

    Emphasize:
    - *Personal language creates a negative impression on the reader.*
    - *Objective and impersonal writing has more authority because it implies neutrality, compared with individual, subjective, personal opinions.*

2. Use of outside sources

Option 1

1. Write the following question on the board:
   - *What rules do you remember about using outside sources?*

2. Have students work in pairs or small groups to discuss the question.

3. Elicit answers and write them on the board.

Option 2

1. Have students read questions 1, 2, and 3 and the points under each, page 125.

2. As students are reading, write the following questions on the board:
   - *What are three patterns of in-text citation?*
   - *How can you avoid plagiarism?*
   - *What are the rules regarding using quotations?*

3. With books closed, have students in pairs or small groups discuss the questions.

4. Elicit answers and write them on the board.

5. Confirm answers.
   (Answers)
   - **In-text citation – See pages 90–91.**
   - **Plagiarism – By paraphrasing, summarizing, and quoting.**
   - **Quotations – See pages 85–88.**

3. Grammar, punctuation, spelling, capitalization

1. Write the following question on the board:
   - *What would you think if you read an essay filled with grammar, punctuation, spelling, and capitalization mistakes?*

2. Have students work in pairs or small groups to discuss the questions.

3. Elicit answers and write them on the board.

4. Confirm answer. (Example answer: **People would likely think 1) this essay is annoying to read, and 2) the writer was too lazy to even fix small mistakes, so why should I read it?**)

5. Have students read the explanation in the textbook.

6. Emphasize:
   - *Not being a native English speaker is not an excuse for submitting an essay filled with small mistakes. Most universities have a writing center or some other assistance to help students correct these small mistakes, so those resources should be used.*

Section 3 Editing by another person

1. Write the following question on the board:
   - *What are the benefits of having an outside person edit your essay?*

2. Have students work in pairs or small groups to discuss the question.

3. Elicit answers and write them on the board.

4. Confirm answer.
   (Answer)
   Another person can:
   - **offer a fresh perspective on the essay, and**
   - **give a more objective opinion on how effective and comprehensible the essay is.**

5. Have students read the explanation in the textbook, page 126.

6. Then have students look at the editing checklists on pages 126–127.

7. Emphasize:
   - *The two editing checklists have two columns on the right – one for the writer and the other for an outside person. Regardless of how many times an essay has been self-edited, the final edit should be the result of an outside person's feedback on the essay.*
   - *The teacher is not the only person with the authority to edit an essay. It is most likely that editing by another person will be done by a classmate. Classmates are a useful source of feedback because:*
     - *they will probably have some knowledge on the essay topic.*
     - *they will probably be able to suggest other information that could be included in the essay.*

Exercise 1

Edit one paragraph at a time and follow any option below. Editing the entire essay without an answer check until the end may be difficult for students. The exercise could also be assigned as homework.

Also have students edit the References list, which has mistakes. The mistakes in the references are both the source details in the incorrect position, and missing information. Students can either correct the mistakes with only the details provided, or be asked to actually find the sources on the internet and add the missing details.

Option 1

1. Have students work individually to complete the exercise.

2. When done, have students compare answers with a partner.

3. Elicit answers.

Option 2

1. Divide the class into pairs or small groups.

2. Have students work collaboratively to complete the exercise.

3. Elicit answers.

Option 3

1. Follow steps one and two of Option 2 above.

2. Re-divide students into new pairs or groups so they are sitting with at least one new person.

3. Have them compare their answers with each other.

4. Elicit answers.

   Emphasize:
   - *Even after the course is over, keep the textbook as a resource and refer to it whenever writing an essay.*

Answer Key

UNIT 1 PART 1

Exercise 1

p. 4

Recall:

Summarize the most significant theories of early twentieth century psychologists and how they revolutionized the field of psychology.

Describe the American judicial system and how it is designed to limit wrongful convictions.

Define the term "success" using points from the various assigned readings on Buddhism.

Analysis:

Analyze the growth of Apple's market share since the introduction of the iMac.

Discuss some of the advances in twentieth century technology which have helped transform the workplace.

Compare the health care systems of France and the United States.

Synthesis:

Using points from the various readings assigned this semester, determine the most critical turning points in the evolution of human societies.

Watch the film *Mulholland Drive* and identify its "film noir" characteristics. Refer to the aspects of the classic movies from the 1950s covered in the lecture.

Evaluation:

Evaluate the effectiveness of anti-piracy laws on curbing the illegal downloading of digitalized video, music, and print.

Argue for or against the expansion of the school week from five to seven days.

Exercise 2

p. 5

1. Select several of Picasso's paintings representing both his pre- and post-war periods. Compare aspects of both periods. Explain the transformations which occurred in his art, making sure to refer to color, images, and expressions.

   Select several of Picasso's paintings from both his pre- and post-war periods.
   - Compare aspects of both periods.
   - Explain the transformations which occurred in his art.
     - Refer to color, images, and expressions.

2. The lectures in this course have thus far focused on the 30 articles in the U.N. Declaration of Human Rights and the historical basis for each. Select one of the Declaration's member countries and describe the challenges it faces in trying to uphold the human rights standards outlined in the articles. Determine how close the country is to being a model human rights state.

   Select one of the Declaration's member countries.
   - Describe the challenges it faces in trying to uphold the human rights standards outlined in the articles.
   - Determine how close the country is to being a model human rights state.

3. In the class, examples were given of how socio-cultural factors affect the perception of certain issues which often lead to misunderstandings and breakdowns in diplomatic negotiations, protests, and even armed conflicts. Select a particular issue which eventually led to an armed conflict. Contrast how this issue may have been perceived on both sides of the conflict, making sure to include points on differing values, beliefs, behavior, and laws.

   Select a particular issue which eventually led to an armed conflict.
   - Contrast how this issue may have been perceived on both sides of the conflict.
     - Include points on differing values, beliefs, behavior, and laws.

4. Analyze a contemporary novel with a female protagonist and compare and contrast it with classic works where women were traditionally portrayed as the villain or victim, such as in the works analyzed in the course (e.g., *Macbeth*, *The Scarlet Letter*, *The Great Gatsby*, *Washington Square*). Be sure to a) comment on whether or not women still come across as being the "weaker sex" in more modern literature, and b) identify where symbolism and allegory are used in defining the woman's character.

   Analyze a contemporary novel with a female protagonist.
   - Compare and contrast it with classic works where women were traditionally portrayed as the villain or the victim.
     - Comment on whether or not women still come across as being the "weaker sex" in more modern literature.
   - Identify where symbolism and allegory are used in defining the woman's character.

UNIT 1 PART 2

Exercise 1

p. 9

(Example answers)

1. The invention of portable computers and wireless internet access has radically altered both where and when people can work.

    The invention of database software and electronic storage have revolutionized the workplace by giving employees immediate access to information and facilitating simple information organization.

    Climate control systems and refrigeration have enabled employees to work longer hours, significantly improved productivity, and boosted physical well-being.

2. Despite having different sources of funding, both health care systems have found ways to provide some of the world's most cutting edge medical care.

    The health care system of the United States is less egalitarian than that of France in terms of access to treatment.

    The differences in health care systems in the United States and France reflect differences in general ideas in both countries about the role government should play in the lives of citizens.

3. Anti-piracy laws have done little to prevent piracy from occurring.

    Anti-piracy laws, while imperfect, do offer a deterrent to many around the world.

    Anti-piracy laws have proven to be relatively effective in preventing illegal downloading.

4. Expanding the school week to seven days is necessary to ensure students remain competitive in an increasingly globalized economy.

    Expanding the school week to seven days would be detrimental to children's mental, physical, and social development.

    Although expanding the school week seems necessary, adding only one more day to the school week seems like a more reasonable choice than making children go to school every day.

5. The instant nature of social networking sites has encouraged people to become more open with their thoughts and feelings.

    The expanded friendship networks provided by social networking sites have allowed people to maintain a wider circle of acquaintances.

    Certain social networking sites have become important tools in the way people find jobs and earn an income.

6. The increasing popularity of shows about crime laboratories reflects society's increasing fascination with and belief in technology's ability to solve societal ills.

The popularity of reality television may reflect society's boredom with the mundane and a desire to live a more exciting life.

The enduring popularity of medical dramas perhaps shows audiences' hopes that illnesses and disease can be overcome.

UNIT 1 PART 3

Exercise 1

p. 12

(Example answers)

1. How has the workplace changed in the twentieth century?

    Do people communicate differently?

    Has their working environment changed?

    What tasks have become more efficient?

    What changes have been tied to technology?

    Did certain changes result from one technological advance or from a combination of technological advances?

    Are there statistics I can find which can quantify the changes before and after the advance?

    Have there been any negative effects from technological advances?

2. How are the health care systems similar and different:
    - Cost?
    - Funding?
    - How much doctors are paid?
    - Level of care between rich and poor?

    How do people in the two countries feel about their health care system?

    What are some criticisms of both systems?

    Is the structure of the health care system related to the culture of the country?

    Which population is healthier?

3. What laws currently exist?

    What laws have been made recently?

    Has illegal downloading decreased after these laws were made?

    What are the penalties?

    How are the laws enforced?

    What would happen if anti-piracy laws didn't exist?

    What do supporters of anti-piracy laws argue?

    What do opponents of anti-piracy laws argue?

    Have there been other solutions proposed to reduce illegal downloading?

4. Are there any countries with a seven-day school week? If so, how do their students perform compared with students in countries with a five-day school week?

   Have there been schools that were able to improve student performance without extending the week?

   Is there a relationship between the amount of time students spend at school and their performance on tests?

   Is there evidence of the psychological effects of constant schooling?

   Should parents be worried about burnout? Does having a break aid in the learning process?

   How much more could students learn if they went to school seven days each week?

   What do experts in favor of a seven-day school week say?

   What do experts against a seven-day school week say?

5. What significant developments in social networking have occurred?

   What are the top social networking sites?

   How many people use social networking sites?

   How much time do people spend on social networking sites?

   Have certain aspects of people's lives been more affected than others?

   What are some of the criticisms of social networking?

   Is it easier to stay in touch with more people? How did people stay in contact before these developments?

   Has social networking reduced the amount of "face" time with people?

   Has the way people network to find jobs changed?

6. What are some TV shows which are currently popular (i.e., what are the current TV ratings)?

   How are television shows now different from TV shows in the past?

   What societal changes have happened to make these shows popular?

   Are particular types of shows popular, or are people's tastes diverse?

   How much is real life represented in shows?

   Have certain shows been popular for a long time? What value/values could this be connected to?

Exercise 2

p. 15

(Example answers)
Research information:

Torness nuclear reactor CO_2 emissions = 5g/kWh, coal plant = 900g/kWh

Nuclear reactor's greenhouse gas emissions lower than wind and solar power

Synthesis Statement:

In terms of CO_2 emissions, nuclear power is actually a greener option than other energy sources.

Research information:

Chernobyl, 1986, 31 immediate deaths . . .

Fatalities: coal extractions – 20,000, hydropower – 30,0000

Synthesis Statement:

Although not without risks, nuclear reactors are a relatively safe means of generating power.

Research information:

Nuclear energy preferred in Asia

After Fukushima, suspension/canceling new nuclear plants "merely a knee-jerk reaction . . ."

301 new reactors under construction

Stable sources of uranium available from Canada or Australia

Synthesis Statement:

Despite recent calls for its eradication, nuclear power remains a necessary and sustainable means by which to meet world energy demand.

Research information:

- Solar power – expensive solar panels
- As solar power costs fall, will lead to increase at local level
- One hour of sun's power = human energy needs for a year
- If innovation increased, solar can produce more energy

Synthesis Statement:

In time, solar power will likely be responsible for a much more significant share of the world's energy portfolio, but for now it remains too expensive and is inadequate to meet the world's energy needs.

Exercise 3

p. 16

NOTE: This is the recommended answer based on the information in Exercise 2, but the position could be different if students have differing personal interpretations of the information.

- Nuclear energy should be mostly relied on.

UNIT 1 PART 4

Exercise 1

p. 19

1. c

   a is incorrect because it makes an evaluation of the judicial system (better than most) which is not required in the prompt.

   b is incorrect because it simply states that wrongful convictions are eliminated, not the ways the system limits wrongful convictions.

2. b

   a is incorrect because it describes box office performance, not "film noir" characteristics.

   c is incorrect because it evaluates the film (confusing) rather than relating it to classic "film noir."

3. c

   a is incorrect because it does not specify any turning points.

   b is incorrect because it describes the present rather than a past turning point.

4. c

   a is incorrect because it is a subjective evaluation (best country in the world) which is not required by the essay prompt, and it does not describe "challenges."

   b is incorrect because it does not select a particular member country.

Exercise 2

p. 22

OUTLINE

Thesis:
Despite fears over its safety, nuclear energy still seems to be the only option to sufficiently meet the demands of an increasingly energy-hungry world while limiting damage to the environment.

Main argument 1:
One benefit of nuclear power is that it is a much cleaner and safer energy source than fossil fuels.

Supporting points:
- **some think not safe, but unreasonable; other energy more deaths**
- **emits low CO_2**

Main argument 2:
Another appeal of nuclear power is that the cost of production is extremely low for such an efficient energy source.

Supporting points:
- **cheaper than natural gas and oil**
- **building nuclear power plants is expensive, but over time still cheaper**
- **renewable energy – innovation still needed to make cheaper and more available**
- **any energy source is expensive**

Main argument 3:
Another reason nuclear power should be a significant part of the world's energy supply is its reliability.

Supporting points:
- **production of nuclear energy is constant**
- **nuclear energy – reliability of suppliers**
- **renewable energy has potential, but not enough; erratic supply**

NUCLEAR POWER:
A viable means of meeting our future energy demands

One way to measure a country's economic and social development
is its increased usage of and reliance on energy. Most people now heat or
cool their homes, cook, wash, power their TV or computer, and commute
using energy mostly derived from fossil fuels. Our ancestors who lived
as recently as 100 years ago would marvel at how much energy is used
now and taken for granted. However, as the world's population has
surpassed seven billion, and a growing proportion are seeing big increases
in their wealth and energy consumption, achieving energy sufficiency
while minimizing environmental damage is a challenging but crucial
task. Undoubtedly, the key to environmental sustainability is curbing
the overuse of and dependency on environmentally damaging fossil fuels
like coal, natural gas, and oil. Many believe that increasing the reliance
on nuclear power – a relatively clean, cheap, and reliable form of energy
– is the answer. It contributes a vital 13.4% of the world's energy supply
(International Energy Agency, 2011), and in Asia, a region where nuclear
energy is in favor (Chang & Thomson, 2011), 301 new reactors are either
under construction, planned, or proposed (World Nuclear Association,
2010). Others, wary of the potential risks of nuclear power, see a solution
in harnessing the power available through natural sources such as wind
or sunlight. Yet, while such renewable forms of energy have incredible
potential and have recently seen increased investment and innovation,
none of them have been shown to be able to produce energy on a level
anywhere close to that currently being consumed around the world.
Therefore, at least for the time being, despite fears over its safety, nuclear
energy seems to be the only viable option for satisfying the demands
of an increasingly energy-hungry world while limiting damage to the
environment.

One benefit of nuclear power is that it is a much cleaner and
safer energy source than fossil fuels. Nuclear energy emits virtually no
environmentally harmful carbon. British Energy (2005) asserts that the
total CO_2 emissions from the Torness nuclear reactor in Scotland are
estimated to be just over 5 grams per kilowatt hour (g/kWh), compared
to the 900 g/kWh produced by a coal plant (p. 6). Indeed, research by
the International Energy Agency (2011) showed that greenhouse gas
emissions over a nuclear reactor's lifecycle are actually lower than what
wind or solar power would emit over a similar period at a similar wattage.
It is apparent then that nuclear energy has a crucial part to play in lowering
the world's carbon emissions and safeguarding the environment. Its critics,
however, question whether nuclear energy is especially clean, given the
necessity of storing radioactive waste nuclear power produces, and the
potential release of harmful levels of radiation through nuclear accidents.

The Chernobyl accident in 1986 led to 31 fatalities, and subsequently many more radiation-related deaths (Nuclear Energy Institute, 2011). The environmental and human cost of the nuclear leaks in 2011 from a reactor in Fukushima, Japan, after it was hit by a tsunami, is still being quantified. Incidents such as these ignite fears over nuclear safety, leading to fierce resistance by the public in certain countries towards building new reactors. For many, the risks of increasing the use of nuclear power outweigh any advantages. However, it seems unreasonable to equate these two disasters with nuclear plants everywhere. By far, the vast majority of the world's nuclear plants are not at risk from a tsunami, and the rigorous prevention, monitoring, and containment procedures in reactors now virtually eliminate the likelihood of another Chernobyl-like accident (Nuclear Energy Institute, 2011). It is also a mistake to believe other energy sources are entirely safe. Between 1969 and 2000, fatalities from coal extraction numbered over 20,000, and hydropower generation accounted for approximately 30,000 deaths, dwarfing the number of fatalities from nuclear disasters (Nuclear Energy Agency, 2010). In addition to public concerns about dangerous emissions, worries have also been expressed over what happens with waste from plants.

The fear over nuclear waste is commonly misunderstood. According to Cambridge University physics professor David MacKay (2008), nuclear power produces about 760 ml of radioactive waste per person, per year, that must be securely stored for about 1,000 years. Of this amount, however, only about 25 ml is actually dangerous. This amount is minute compared to the other wastes humans produce each year, including 517 kgs of garbage, and 83 kgs of hazardous industrial waste per person. Correspondingly, the amount of land required to store garbage and dangerous toxic waste is much larger and, due to its threats to both the environment and human health, much of the waste must be securely isolated from its surroundings. Given that society already tolerates having to deal with such a massive amount of hazardous waste, exercising similar precautions for equally dangerous but far less abundant nuclear waste does not seem to warrant special concern. Hopefully, careful consideration of these facts will lead the general public to recognize nuclear power's advantages in terms of cleanliness and safety. Indeed, it should be a significant part of any country's plans to reduce its dependence on fossil fuels.

Another appeal of nuclear power is that the cost of production is extremely low for such an efficient energy source. With energy demands increasing, producing enough energy is vital, and keeping costs low is necessary for making sure energy remains affordable. The U.N. Secretary-General, Bani Ki-Moon, in addressing the world's growing population, has consistently emphasized the necessity of supplying the poor with cheap electricity (United Nations Population Fund, 2011) – and few forms of electricity come cheaper than nuclear energy. Nuclear energy can be produced at 2.14 cents per kilowatt hour (kWh), compared with natural gas (4.86 cents per kWh), and oil (15.18 cents per kWh) (Nuclear

Energy Institute, 2010). Essentially, the many parts of the world eager to become less reliant on fossil fuels are unlikely to find a more cost-effective alternative to nuclear energy. ❶ / ❸ However, many claim that the expense of building nuclear power plants makes nuclear energy far more expensive than one might assume for the cost of energy generation. ❷ The huge cost of planning, designing, and funding nuclear power plants, critics assert, as well as the length of time required to achieve fully functioning power plants (given how politically fraught the issue is), means nuclear energy is a prohibitively expensive enterprise. ❷ A proposed nuclear reactor in Britain is estimated to cost $7.9 billion (Nuclear power: Nukes of hazard, ❹ 2011), which is a massive outlay at a time when government budgets are ❶ stretched. But as Kimura (2011) stresses, although the initial expense of nuclear power is extremely high, once the plants are functioning, this cost is not so significant when divided by the years the station will be ❷ generating electricity. In contrast, *The Economist* notes that solar power use remains largely confined to individuals who can afford the expensive solar panels, or to companies able to buy the many expensive panels and the large amount of land required to create solar farms (Solar power, 2011). It is hoped that as solar power costs fall, and its ability to generate ❸ sufficient electricity increases, its acceptance and adoption at the local level will increase greatly (Roaf & Gupta, 2007; MacKay, 2008). Yet, as development of the technology is slow and incremental, this seems a long way off. Radical breakthroughs are necessary to make renewable energy as widely available and cheap as nuclear power is now. Therefore, while renewable energy has undeniable promise, nuclear energy remains the ❶ most viable, available energy source for a world with an ever-increasing appetite for energy.

A further reason why nuclear power should be a significant part of ❶ / ❷ the world's energy supply is its reliability. Once nuclear power plants ❷ are built and functioning, the production of nuclear energy is constant. Wind and solar power, however, are intermittent energy producers. Wind ❸ turbines are not much use when there is no wind, while solar power has limited potential in, say, cloud-covered Northern Europe. A key advantage ❸ of nuclear power is that, come gale, rain or shine, nuclear energy is still generated. Nuclear power plants can also depend on having a stable supply ❷ of materials. Oil and gas are currently produced in relatively unstable regions of the world, which makes an over-reliance on this energy source risky to the extent that it could jeopardize national security. Accordingly, as Moran and Russell (2009) point out, issues of energy security are now ❸ high on the agendas of political leaders throughout the world. In contrast, the primary source of nuclear power – uranium – is easily supplied by Canada and Australia, two comparatively stable countries (Nuclear power: Nukes of hazard, 2011). With the regular supply of uranium guaranteed, ❶ / ❷ nuclear energy can be generated domestically at constant levels, forming the basis of a country's security and self-reliance. Many argue, though, that certain renewable energy forms that safely harness the earth's natural ❸ energy could become more reliable. Wind power is proving to be a growing, domestically generated, energy source. Solar power is even more promising: one hour of the sun's power contains more than humanity's energy needs for one year (Solar power, 2011). With increasing technical advances, its supporters claim, solar power can be responsible for a much greater share of energy production (Tanaka, 2010). However, despite the clear potential of such forms of energy, if nuclear energy generation were to cease immediately, renewable sources, given their current erratic nature, would be unable to meet the 13.4% required to make up the deficit. As the world tries to gradually move away from its reliance on fossil fuels, nuclear power still remains the only energy supply constant enough to depend on for an adequate supply of energy.

❸

❹

❶

It is apparent that nuclear power does offer a realistic means of meeting the world's growing energy demands, while at the same time limiting environmental destruction. Nuclear energy is clean and cheap, its production is reliable, and its materials are readily available. However, as a result of several major nuclear accidents, the public is wary of potential disasters on their doorstep, making nuclear power a currently unpopular choice. On the other hand, renewable energy, which is far more accepted and much easier to champion, remains unable to provide a significant share of the world's energy needs. Perhaps in the future the huge potential of solar, wind, or some other form of renewable energy will be unlocked, allowing it to power all that fossil fuels power now. Until then, governments and the nuclear energy industry should make the case for nuclear energy more aggressively to appease a nervous but seemingly misinformed public about the role nuclear power plays in making life comfortable for so many around the world.

❶

❷

❸

❶

UNIT 2 PART 1

Exercise 1

p. 33

NUCLEAR POWER:
A viable means of meeting our future energy demands

One way to measure a country's economic and social development is its increased usage of and reliance on energy. Most people now heat or cool their homes, cook, wash, power their TV or computer, and commute using energy mostly derived from fossil fuels. Our ancestors who lived as recently as 100 years ago would marvel at how much energy is used now and taken for granted. However, as the world's population has surpassed seven billion, and a growing proportion are seeing big increases in their wealth and energy consumption, achieving energy sufficiency while minimizing environmental damage is a challenging but crucial task. Undoubtedly, the key to environmental sustainability is curbing the overuse of and dependency on environmentally damaging fossil fuels

History/
current situation

like coal, natural gas, and oil. Many believe that increasing the reliance on nuclear power – a relatively clean, cheap, and reliable form of energy – is the answer. It contributes a vital 13.4% of the world's energy supply (International Energy Agency, 2011), and in Asia, a region where nuclear energy is in favor (Chang & Thomson, 2011), 301 new reactors are either under construction, planned, or proposed (World Nuclear Association, 2010). Others, wary of the potential risks of nuclear power, see a solution in harnessing the power available through natural sources such as wind or sunlight. Yet, while such renewable forms of energy have incredible potential and have recently seen increased investment and innovation, none of them have been shown to be able to produce energy on a level anywhere close to that currently being consumed around the world. Therefore, at least for the time being, despite fears over its safety, nuclear energy seems to be the only viable option for satisfying the demands of an increasingly energy-hungry world while limiting damage to the environment.

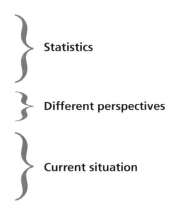

Statistics

Different perspectives

Current situation

Exercise 2

p. 34

(Example answers)

1. **Background:**
   - Contemporary perceptions about marriage/ portrayal in popular culture
   - Notion of arranged marriage as "backwards" by some
   - Statistics about arranged marriages in various countries
   - Assumptions about the success rates of arranged marriages, and how these assumptions are unfounded

2. **Background:**
   - Information about the "global village" and the diversity of information available on the internet
   - Examples of information which has prompted racist/ethnocentrist reactions
   - Statistics about racism/enthnocentrism in the past vs. now
   - Assumptions about how exposure to other cultures increases open-mindedness, and a challenge to those assumptions

3. **Background:**
   - Information about well-known major technological developments in the twenty-first century
   - Clarification for readers about what nanotechnology is
   - A few notable examples of inventions/ breakthroughs made possible by nanotechnology

4. **Background:**
   - How notions about what is physically attractive have changed throughout history
   - Information about how society has changed over the past 30 years
   - Information about two seemingly opposite male or female actors, one from the past and another from the present, starting with an emphasis on the obvious differences before surprising the reader by looking more closely for similarities

5. **Background:**
   - Statistics about increasing drug use and how much money has been spent combating it
   - Information about what drug use is likely to look like in the future if nothing has changed
   - Information about current tactics, followed by some of the "radical tactics" that have been suggested

p. 37

NOTE: Either of the underlined parts below can be considered a motive. A motive may fit into more than one category.

NUCLEAR POWER:
A viable means of meeting our future energy demands

One way to measure a country's economic and social development is its increased usage of and reliance on energy. Most people now heat or cool their homes, cook, wash, power their TV or computer, and commute using energy mostly derived from fossil fuels. Our ancestors who lived as recently as 100 years ago would marvel at how much energy is used now and taken for granted. However, <u>as the world's population has surpassed seven billion, and a growing proportion are seeing big increases in their wealth and energy consumption, achieving energy sufficiency while minimizing environmental damage is a challenging but crucial task</u>. Undoubtedly, the key to environmental sustainability is curbing the overuse of and dependency on environmentally damaging fossil fuels like coal, natural gas, and oil. Many believe that increasing the reliance on nuclear power – a relatively clean, cheap, and reliable form of energy – is the answer. It contributes a vital 13.4% of the world's energy supply (International Energy Agency, 2011), and in Asia, a region where nuclear energy is in favor (Chang & Thomson, 2011), 301 new reactors are either under construction, planned, or proposed (World Nuclear Association, 2010). <u>Others, wary of the potential risks of nuclear power, see a solution in harnessing the power available through natural sources such as wind or sunlight. Yet, while such renewable forms of energy have incredible potential and have recently seen increased investment and innovation, none of them have been shown to be able to produce energy on a level anywhere close to that currently being consumed around the world.</u> Therefore, at least for the time being, despite fears over its safety, nuclear energy seems to be the only viable option for satisfying the demands of an increasingly energy-hungry world while limiting damage to the environment.

Exercise 4

p. 38

NOTE: Either of the two parts below can be considered a motive.

a. Much has been written about the cultural basis of seniority-based versus merit-based promotion and pay in companies, as well as the benefits and drawbacks of each system. <u>A seniority-based system is more common in the East – e.g., Thailand, Japan – where the hard work and loyalty of company employees are rewarded with increased status and pay as they get older. While such a system virtually guarantees lifetime employment for employees, it also often breeds inefficiency and even laziness among those who feel there is no incentive to do more than what is required of their position.</u>  A merit-based system, however, is prevalent in the West – e.g., the United States, the U.K. – where productivity is the basis of position and pay. <u>It gives employees the incentive to work hard and be innovative, but it also often leads to competition among employees, resulting in distrust and conflict in the workplace as well as less job security.</u> Studies have indicated that there seems to be a shift toward a more merit-based system among companies in the East, but a number of factors can help determine if such a shift is necessary or desirable.

Type 2 or 3 is possible.

Type 2 – Problem: laziness; Type 3 – The writer thinks understanding the factors introduced in the essay will be helpful in making the choice between a merit-based and a seniority-based system.

b. Since the middle of the twentieth century, Keynesian economic theory has been the mainstay of governmental policies in regulating the economy. The theory essentially contends that in times of recession, a free-market economy may not be able to self-correct naturally, thereby requiring the government to intervene by trying to stimulate the economy with such measures as tax and interest rate cuts and increases in spending on various projects. <u>Although Keynesian policy has been successful in the sense that there has not yet been a repeat of the Great Depression of 1929, the lingering effects of the market collapse of 2007–8 and subsequent recessions have shown that traditional government interventions are having relatively little effect in turning economies around.</u> An explanation for this lies in examining particular aspects of modern communication, especially with regard to the effect of the media and "bandwagon" behavior.

Type 3 – The writer will explain societal factors that limit the effect of Keynesian-type government intervention in a depressed economy.

c. <u>Much credit is given to Hollywood for spreading American culture around the world through movies and TV shows. However, one might argue that another American export has had an equally or even more pervasive effect in capturing the minds and souls of people worldwide: hip-hop.</u> Hip-hop culture began on the streets of New York in the 1970s, as house and street parties in black and Hispanic communities provided a venue for listening to rap music and wearing loose-fitting brand sportswear as a fashion statement. Since then, hip-hop has won fans around the world, as youths have adopted its musical, clothing, and speaking styles, while also combining elements of their own culture. There are a number of factors which have driven hip-hop's popularity and helped create one of the world's truly global music styles.

Type 3 – The writer wants to explain why hip-hop has achieved global success.

Exercise 5

p. 39

(Example answers)

a. Scientific evidence has recently exonerated people who were convicted on the basis of witness testimony, but witness testimony is still considered a valid form of evidence in trials.

b. Many people assume the best way to prevent traffic accidents is to increase the number of rules and restrictions. However, having to pay attention to too many things at once could actually distract drivers, increasing the potential for accidents.

c. Countries around the world spend huge amounts of money in what are usually failed bids to host the Olympics. In fact, it might appear absurd to many in society to spend so much money in an attempt to secure something that will cost even more in promotion and construction costs.

d. Doctors in many developed countries discount traditional remedies as unreliable and dangerous because of a lack of biological research supporting their effectiveness. However, though their mechanisms are not yet fully understood, new research has shown that many traditional remedies are actually effective in treating a variety of ailments.

e. As health care improves, costs are soaring, putting excessive strain on government spending. However, many chronic diseases, which are also often the most expensive to treat, are a result of poor lifestyle choices.

UNIT 2 PART 2

Exercise 1

p. 43

1. As of 2008, over half of the people using a social networking system were over 35 years old.

    Not effective: A specific factual statement; does not seem to require supporting sentences.

2. First, cars are safer today than ever before because airbags have become a standard safety feature.

    Effective: Topic and controlling idea are clear; supporting sentences should support how airbags have increased safety.

3. Furthermore, although not an old technology, they have already become obsolete.

    Not effective: Topic is not clearly stated.

4. Increased productivity in the workplace has been another result of staff being allowed to use their own tablet computers.

    Effective: Topic and controlling idea are clear; supporting sentences should show how having tablet computers helps increase productivity.

5. Another limitation is that electricity cannot be generated at night.

    Not effective: Topic is not clearly stated.

Exercise 2

p. 43

1. **Thesis:**
    Certain aspects of reality TV shows reflect the American character and preferences, which enable these programs to dominate television ratings in the U.S.

    Potential topic sentences:

    a. Reality TV has also caught on in Asia, so much so that they have started their own shows there which are similar or even direct copies of the original American versions.

        No (The controlling idea is not related to the thesis about these shows reflecting the American character and preferences.)

    b. Many of the participants in the most popular reality TV shows are there to achieve status and prestige, which is indicative of what motivates Americans in general in many aspects of their life.

        Yes (Achieving status and prestige are aspects of the American character, so this topic sentence is relevant to the thesis.)

    c. Almost every major TV network in the U.S. has its own lineup of reality TV shows, with new ones debuting every season.

        No (The thesis is not about the TV networks or how many reality shows they produce.)

    d. Reality TV also highlights the competitive nature of Americans, as many shows have features which make them as dramatic as sports events.

        Yes (The shows having drama similar to a sporting event indicates a preference for competition, which is directly related to the American character.)

2. **Thesis:**
    With society's high value on personal and environmental health, an increasing number of people are becoming vegetarians because of the benefits it brings to individuals and the world's ecosystem.

    Potential topic sentences:

    a. Adopting a vegetarian diet is widely believed to reduce the risk of many illnesses.

        Yes (Reducing the risk of many illnesses is a personal health benefit, so this topic sentence is relevant to the thesis.)

b. Vegetarians used to be known as Pythagoreans, after the ancient Greek philosopher and mathematician Pythagoras, an early advocate of non-meat diets.

No (Information about Pythagoras is irrelevant to personal or environmental health.)

c. A vegetarian lifestyle is also seen as fashionable among some young people.

No (The thesis expresses health benefits, so fashion does not really relate to this idea.)

d. The success of animal rights groups over the last four decades has created a generation expecting the ethical treatment of animals.

Yes (The ethical treatment of animals is a part of how society values environmental health, so this topic sentence indicates the paragraph will detail how this belief has led to more people becoming vegetarians.)

e. Adopting a vegetarian diet is also believed to contribute to a reduction in greenhouse gases that cause global warming.

Yes (Reducing greenhouse gases is related to the thesis' idea of environmental health.)

f. In many Western countries, Asian food has become much more popular due to its perceived health benefits.

No (The topic sentence is about Asian food, not vegetarian food, and about popularity, not personal or environmental benefits.)

g. Another factor is protecting the balance of the world's ecosystem.

No (The controlling idea is related to environmental health, but the topic "another factor" is not specified, so overall the topic sentence is ineffective.)

Exercise 3

p. 49

8 With no investment in infrastructure projects or business ventures, entire regions remain isolated and backwards because of the threat of malaria.

5 This impact on people results in a significant reduction in productivity and lost income, and inhibits daily commercial activity.

9 In all, malaria, a disease seen as a result of poverty, is also a significant contributor to poverty throughout the developing world.

2 First, communicable diseases such as malaria negatively affect the workforce.

7 The World Bank (2007) found that in areas where malaria outbreaks are commonly reported, investment from both domestic and international sources are virtually non-existent.

6 The presence of malaria also prevents larger scale economic development through discouraging investment.

4 Moreover, malaria prevents the many people in developing regions who work from their homes

from participating in the day-to-day commerce of their community.

1 The presence of disease limits the economic growth of many developing countries.

3 The World Health Organization (2010) estimates that malaria alone accounts for nearly 40 percent of absenteeism among workers in developing countries.

Exercise 4

p. 50

(Example answers)

1. **Explanation:** Therefore, shifting towards more nuclear power would aid in minimizing the effects of energy production on global warming.

2. **Claim:** A number of health factors that naturally occur as people get older can influence their ability to drive safely.

   Explanation: Because avoiding many traffic accidents requires the ability to notice a problem, make a decision, and act within a matter of seconds, stricter tests would help guarantee that those unable to act quickly do not get behind the wheel.

Exercise 5

p. 51

(Example answers)

Thesis:
Globalization is essentially Americanization, as U.S. culture has become a part of the daily lives of people in countries around the world.

1. **Topic sentence:** One clear way U.S. culture is expanding globally is through its food.

   Claim: Certain U.S. fast food restaurants can be found in many countries.

   Evidence: McDonald's now operates over 25,000 restaurants worldwide, and opens six new ones per day.

   Explanation: Such a rate of expansion shows that people across the globe are increasingly including American-style meals into their diet, and undoubtedly eating less of their own culture's food.

   OR

   This level of expansion internationally is unmatched by any non-American franchise, and is indicative of U.S. dominance rather than an even exchange of cultures.

2. **Topic sentence:** The U.S. is also permeating cultures around the world through entertainment.

   Claim: Nowhere has this been more evident than in the movie industry.

   Evidence: About two-thirds of movie ticket sales around the world are for films made in the United States.

   Explanation: One possible effect of this is the spread of the lifestyle and attitudes of Americans shown in these films, at times to the point where they are adopted by those in other cultures.

OR
This indicates a possible preference for things American, such as their look, lifestyle, or even attitude.

Exercise 6

p. 53

1.

Paragraph 2
Topic: one of the main problems tourists cause in Antarctica
Controlling idea: disruption of scientific research being conducted there

Paragraph 3
Topic: solution to the problem
Controlling idea: increased cooperation between the tour organizers and researchers

Paragraph 4
Topic: safeguarding scientific efforts in Antarctica
Controlling idea: amounts to very little if tourists can still disrupt the ecosystem

Paragraph 5
Topic: guidelines for tourists
Controlling idea: more needs to be done to ensure guidelines are followed

Paragraph 6
Topic: Antarctic ecosystem is also threatened
Controlling idea: environmental hazards brought by the increasing stream of tourists

Paragraph 7
No topic sentence – this body paragraph continues the controlling idea in paragraph 6.

Paragraph 8
Topic: addressing the threat of environmental hazards
Controlling idea: coordinated efforts between tour operators, their governments, and the scientists stationed in Antarctica

2.

Paragraph 2

Claim(s): While scientific study in Antarctica was once the main purpose for human presence there, science seems to have given way to tourism.
However, it quickly became apparent that the large number of tourists was beginning to have negative impacts on the scientists.
In addition, scientific staff sometimes have to stop their work to aid tourists who have either ignored the risks or underestimated the extreme conditions of Antarctica.

Evidence: In fact, from 1990, the number of tourists began to increase to a point where their numbers now exceed the number of scientists (Shaik, 2010).
Initially, this was welcomed by research staff whose projects saw a potential funding boost through an increase in visitors, and scientists who stay in Antarctica all year round welcomed the idea of more human contact (Larson, 2012).
According to American University, which funds research in the Antarctic, independent tour companies are often unaware of research schedules and bring hundreds of tourists to scientific sites requesting explanations and tours (Grall, 1992).
They have had to participate in the rescue of pilots who crashed attempting to break records, or other adventurers who were not prepared for the harsh exposure while trekking in the cold (Tourists in Antarctica, 2009).

Explanation:
All of these disruptions take scientists away from their experiments, cost money, delay important results, and potentially endanger their lives.

Paragraph 3
Claim(s): Science-based charities or NGOs can actively promote their research facilities as tourist destinations to ensure minimal interference with research projects.

Evidence: In the Canadian low arctic, for example, a research charity attracts, houses, educates, and leads tourists around the area – all under the supervision of experts at the research station.
The funds generated in doing this finance the charity and its research while completely controlling the impact of tourists (Churchill Northern, 2007).
Likewise, the Chilean government minimizes the impact of tourists who come through their program by confining their visit to its own facilities.
Each facility houses and manages the visitors, and the scientists at each station educate and lead tours based on the research focus of each station (Antarctica annual, 2005).

Explanation: By exercising stricter controls and reducing experimental disruptions, operations such as these seem ideal for properly maintaining a workable balance between research and tourism in Antarctica.

Paragraph 4
Claim(s): The effect that the now nearly 45,000 annual tourists have had on the wildlife in this fragile environment has become a serious concern (Shaik, 2010).
In addition, although a portion claim to have had some environmental sensitivity training prior to departure, the presence of tourists, regardless of whether they venture too close to the animals or stand at a distance, has been proven to cause stress among the wildlife.
Similar problems were also found among animals living in areas frequented by humans, even though these animals are presumed by many to be "used to" tourists.

Evidence: Hoping to view the unique animals of the Antarctic, eco-tourists often venture too closely to their habitats or nesting grounds.
Gene S. Fowler (1999), from the University of Washington, documented elevated levels of adrenalin that Magellanic penguins produced upon being excited or scared by a human.
It took some birds, especially those that saw humans at irregular intervals, months to recover from their symptoms of shock at these encounters.
According to Trathan, Forcada, Atkinson, Downie, and Shears (2008), the presence of too many humans was the likeliest contributor to a significant drop in gentoo penguin breeding in colonies most exposed to tourists.

Explanation: Therefore, tourism's impact on the ecosystem is perhaps even more worrying than its disruptions of ongoing experiments.

The delicate balance of natural cues for animals to nest and mate successfully can be all too easily disturbed by the presence of tourists.

And the resultant population swings, particularly in an environment as fragile as Antarctica, could directly affect the stability of other animal populations connected through the food chain, leading to a vicious cycle that could reverberate throughout the ecosystem.

Paragraph 5

Claim(s): Over the years, researchers have catalogued increasingly numerous incidents of tourists showing either no knowledge of or complete disregard for the visitor guidelines.

Evidence: Tourists often walked dangerously among Weddell seals on the beach, or ventured to within one foot of a penguin's nest for a photo (Grall, 1992; Shaik, 2010), despite the official guidelines of the International Association of Antarctica Tour Operators (IAATO), which advise no closer than 15 feet (Guidelines, 2012).

Similarly, reports of other violations include tourists trying to feed penguins, and numerous incidents of tourists chasing seabirds to make them scatter and fly away for a photo (Trathan et al., 2008).

Explanation: Clearly, the self-regulation of these tour operators is ultimately inadequate in controlling the misdemeanors of tourists.

Therefore, regulation should come from the individual governments of the tour operators.

Licensing of tour operators should depend on how well they enforce the guidelines for behavior among participants in their tours.

Paragraph 6

Claim(s): A number of the tourist cruise ships visiting the area have been damaged by jagged ice, causing oil to gush out into the water.

In addition to that from ships, waste from the numerous research and tourist stations pollutes the land.

Evidence: The Associated Press (2007) reported one notable example of a cruise ship which sank in Antarctic waters, releasing over 210,000 liters of diesel, 24,000 liters of lubricant, and 1,000 liters of gasoline into the surrounding water, threatening thousands of penguins en route to the continent for mating season.

There has been at least one other report of a ship sinking, and several reports of ships coming too close to shore and running aground (Shaik, 2010).

Marcus Zylkstra, an environmentalist in Antarctica, has criticized the condition of a number of American stations as having "decades' worth of human excrement, sewage, gas and oil leaking from broken-down and abandoned vehicles, and numerous piles of discarded garbage and debris" (as cited in Arroyo & Duque, 2004, p. 52).

Explanation: With the presence of more and more vessels, it would only require a few more incidents like these to poison marine life such as krill and plankton, thereby irreparably damaging the food chain.

The extent to which biological and chemical pollutants have continued to find their way into the environment shows the lack of responsibility and coordination by the humans using this fragile land.

Paragraph 7

Claim(s): Moreover, the threat of invasive microbes and other unseen organisms presents a major problem to the safety of the environment.

Evidence: Larson (2012) reports that microbes from foreign environments cling to the boots and jackets of disembarking visitors and infect the flora and fauna in potentially unpredictable ways.

Studies have confirmed that virtually every visitor coming to the region carries a plethora of microscopic life forms alien to Antarctica.

In addition, tourists unknowingly transport tiny seeds which are carried in their clothing (Askin, 2012).

Indeed, Arroyo and Duque (2004) found one invasive species of grass taking root in Antarctica believed to have been introduced via seeds from tourists, and have warned that seeds from "the Iceland Poppy, Tall Fescue Velvet grass and Annual Winter Grass – all from cold climates and capable of growing in Antarctica" (p. 57) have been found, and their spread may threaten the few native grass species.

Snyder (2007) further asserted that native Antarctic grass species are particularly vulnerable because they have never had to compete against other species, so they would be easily overrun by the more aggressive invasive strains.

Explanation: Therefore, introducing even just a few organisms of a foreign species is enough to wreak havoc on the ecosystem.

In total, the potential for a takeover by invasive species combined with the multitude of environmental pollutants unleashed into the Antarctic environment make human activity a real threat to the entire ecological balance of the continent.

Paragraph 8

Claim(s): An alliance between scientists and the tourism industry would aid in facilitating the removal of waste produced by humans.

Formal cooperation between science and tourism could also decrease the chances of the accidental release of foreign microbes.

Individual governments can further aid efforts to stop contamination by making strict licensing requirements for the tour operators.

One especially important requirement is a limit on the number of people allowed to embark on a tour at any one time.

Evidence: The arrival and departure dates could be shared among scientists and tour operators, and tour boats could be responsible for carrying waste with them after they depart.

Tour operators could provide their own outerwear for exclusive use in Antarctica to limit the risk of contamination, and scientists could take further measures to check and disinfect other possessions the tourists might bring.

Many governments already adhere to the established guidelines for scientific cooperation (Australian Antarctic Division, 2011a; Australian Antarctic

Division, 2011b; The Secretariat of the Antarctic Treaty, 2011), and this could act as a basis for all governments involved in Antarctic tourism to cooperatively monitor their tour companies.

Restricting this number would ensure that large ships, which require heavily toxic fuels, are not used in the tours (International Maritime Organization, 2011).

Explanation: Clearly, the regular removal of biological and other waste would reduce the risk of environmental contamination.

Only smaller ships running on lighter and less toxic fuel would be allowed in Antarctic waters, thereby controlling the risk of devastating and irreparable damage to the ecosystem caused by an accident.

3.

Paragraph 3
Topic sentence: A solution to the problem of having scientists attend to the throngs of tourists is increased cooperation between the tour organizers and researchers.

Paragraph 4
Topic sentence: Unfortunately, safeguarding scientific efforts in Antarctica amounts to very little if tourists can still disrupt the ecosystem from which all their data are gathered.

Paragraph 5
Topic sentence: Most tour operators do have guidelines for tourists intended to prevent disruption to the ecosystem, but it is apparent that much more needs to be done to ensure guidelines are followed.

No transitional sentences were used in the essay.

UNIT 2 PART 3

p. 62

Identify the logical fallacy in the following examples.

1. False dichotomy – The author gives two options: the absence of the programs proposed accompanied by an increase in teenage drinking, or the implementation of his/her suggestion, which will bring the problem under control. It seems possible that other strategies might also help solve the problem, and there is not enough evidence that raising awareness would actually work.

2. False cause – The author assumes that the increase of movie violence led to desensitization, which then led to an increase in violent assaults. It seems possible that the increase in violence in films could instead just be reflecting increasing violence in society.

3. Fallacy of division – The author assumes that because one company was not deterred by the possibility of punishment that other companies will behave similarly. More evidence is necessary to show the behavior is widespread and warrants new legislation.

p. 65

1. Slippery slope – The author assumes that poor grades in elementary school math will lead to adults unable to carry out daily tasks in an efficient manner. Although low grades are worrying, it seems possible that most of these students will acquire basic math skills before they become adults. The author's argument would be stronger if he/she could cite studies of the long-term effects of poor performance on math tests in elementary school, and change the argument from making math education "the primary focus of education" to "placing more importance on math education."

2. False appeal – The public consensus does not guarantee that legal boundaries are "fair." The author's argument would be strengthened by more carefully considering the counter-argument and talk about actual negative consequences for society that could arise from harsher penalties.

3. Straw man – The author presents the other side as people who simply hate their country. The argument would be much improved if the author considered and offered a rebuttal to a valid counter-argument for why some people disagree with the proposal.

4. Circular reasoning – The concluding point – that people are attracted to high-scoring sports – is just a repeat of the claim. The argument would be improved if there was an explanation of why high scores are exciting.

5. Non-sequitur – Zoos are not educational because of discounts – this is related to price, not learning. This could be improved if the author explained what students might learn about animals by visiting the zoo.

p. 66

1. **Reason:** Police shot and killed an unarmed man.
   Conclusion: Current training and instruction are inadequate.
   Fallacy of division – It assumes that the actions of one group of police officers (or perhaps one police officer) should determine how police are trained.

2. **Reason:** U.S. military spending accounts for 40 percent of all military spending in the world.
   Conclusion: This has made the U.S. military strong.
   False cause – Although it is possible that a high level of spending has contributed to U.S. military strength, it also seems plausible that a number of other factors, such as training and physical requirements, could also be significant.

3. **Reason:** Cycling is less harmful to the environment than driving.
   Conclusion: People who drive the same distance as those who cycle care less about the environment.
   False dichotomy – It assumes that if someone cares about the environment, he/she will automatically choose cycling. However, a number of other factors, such as safety, weather, or health problems could prevent otherwise environmentally conscious people from cycling to work. In addition, people may be cycling to work for reasons unrelated to the environment.

4. **Reason:** Clare Hall believes that pastel autumn colors are also suitable for casual business environments.
   Conclusion: Companies should change their view of what constitutes business attire.
   False appeal – The opinion presented is just an opinion, and is not supported by any logical reasons for why adopting a different attitude would benefit businesses.

5. **Reason:** Public school teachers are not happy with their working conditions.
   Conclusion: If the government does not increase wages, teachers will quit.
   Non-sequitur – The author seems to believe that "wages" are the only problem teachers have with their working conditions. However, they may have issues related to working hours, health benefits, or the classroom environment.
   OR
   False dichotomy – The writer claims that if the government does not raise wages, teachers will quit, that there is no other action teachers might take.

6. **Reason:** Exam scores have gone up.
   Conclusion: Exams have become easier.
   False cause – The author assumes that the reason students are doing better is because the exam is easier. However, the rise in scores could be due to a number of other factors such as improved study habits, better teachers, or more active parents.

7. **Reason:** Windows is the biggest selling and most widely used computer system.
   Conclusion: Windows is a superior operating system.
   False cause – Although it is possible that people use Windows because it is superior to other products, it also seems possible that its popularity is due to its marketing strategy or because people are reluctant to change operating systems which they are accustomed to.
   OR
   False appeal – Popularity itself is not a reason why the operating system is good.

8. **Reason:** Four of the top 20 largest economies are in Asia.
   Conclusion: Exports are vital to the economies of these countries.

Fallacy of division – Although exports are an important part of many major economies, just because four countries in the region are large exporters does not necessarily mean other Asian countries also rely on exports.
OR
Non-sequitur – It is not immediately clear that these countries' GDP depends on exports. More data is necessary.

9. **Reason:** Illegal downloading has increased and revenues from CD sales have dropped steadily.
   Conclusion: Reducing illegal downloading will cause CD sales to increase.
   False cause – The author is assuming that increased opportunities for illegal downloading is responsible for the drop in CD sales, though there could be a number of other reasons such as the purchase of MP3s or a downturn in the economy.

10. **Reason:** 30 percent of edible food is wasted annually.
    Conclusion: Reducing waste will help feed the starving poor.
    Non-sequitur – It is not immediately clear whether a reduction of food wasted in one part of the world will make more food available to another part of the world. Reducing food waste could simply mean people eating less food, not that they are sending the food that would otherwise be wasted to developing countries.

UNIT 2 PART 4

Exercise 1

p. 71

(Example answers)
1. Companies making such a transition must consider how to proceed in a way that minimizes the shock which workers will inevitably feel.

2. Without this action, governments risk an economy that will reach a state which will be extremely difficult to recover from.

3. So long as young people are struggling to find a voice in society, hip-hop can provide an outlet that transcends language and geography.

UNIT 3 PART 1

Exercise 1

p. 75

Paragraph 2:
In fact, from 1990, the number of tourists began to increase to a point where their numbers now exceed the number of scientists (Shaik, 2010). **(Secondary)**
Initially, this was welcomed by research staff whose projects saw a potential funding boost through an increase in visitors, and scientists who stay in Antarctica all year round welcomed the idea of more human contact (Larson, 2012). **(Secondary)**
According to American University, which funds research in the Antarctic, independent tour companies are often unaware of research schedules and bring hundreds of tourists to scientific sites requesting explanations and tours (Grall, 1992). **(Secondary)**
They have had to participate in the rescue of pilots who crashed attempting to break records, or other adventurers who were not prepared for the harsh exposure while trekking in the cold (Tourists in Antarctica, 2009). **(Secondary)**

Paragraph 3:
The funds generated in doing this finance the charity and its research while completely controlling the impact of tourists (Churchill Northern, 2007). **(Primary)**
Each facility houses and manages the visitors, and the scientists at each station educate and lead tours based on the research focus of each station (Antarctica annual, 2005). **(Secondary)**

Paragraph 4:
The effect that the now nearly 45,000 annual tourists have had on the wildlife in this fragile environment has become a serious concern (Shaik,2010). **(Secondary)**
Gene S. Fowler (1999), from the University of Washington, documented elevated levels of adrenalin that Magellanic penguins produced upon being excited or scared by a human. **(Primary)**
According to Trathan, Forcada, Atkinson, Downie, and Shears (2008), the presence of too many humans was the likeliest contributor to a significant drop in gentoo penguin breeding in colonies most exposed to tourists. **(Primary)**

Paragraph 5:
Tourists often walked dangerously among Weddell seals on the beach, or ventured to within one foot of a penguin's nest for a photo (Grall, 1992; Shaik, 2010), **(Secondary)**
despite the official guidelines of the International Association of Antarctica Tour Operators (IAATO), which advise no closer than 15 feet (Guidelines, 2012). **(Primary)**
Similarly, reports of other violations include tourists trying to feed penguins, and numerous incidents of tourists chasing seabirds to make them scatter and fly away for a photo (Trathan et al., 2008). **(Primary)**

Paragraph 6:
The Associated Press (2007) reported one notable example of a cruise ship which sank in Antarctic waters, releasing over 210,000 liters of diesel, 24,000 liters of lubricant, and 1,000 liters of gasoline into the surrounding water, threatening thousands of penguins en route to the continent for mating season. **(Primary)**
There has been at least one other report of a ship sinking, and several reports of ships coming too close to shore and running aground (Shaik, 2010). **(Secondary)**
Marcus Zylkstra, an environmentalist in Antarctica, has criticized the condition of a number of American stations as having "decades' worth of human excrement, sewage, gas and oil leaking from broken-down and abandoned vehicles, and numerous piles of discarded garbage and debris" (as cited in Arroyo & Duque, 2004, p. 52). **(Secondary)**

Paragraph 7:
Larson (2012) reports that microbes from foreign environments cling to the boots and jackets of disembarking visitors and infect the flora and fauna in potentially unpredictable ways. **(Primary)**
Studies have confirmed that virtually every visitor coming to the region carries a plethora of microscopic life forms alien to Antarctica. In addition, tourists unknowingly transport tiny seeds which are carried in their clothing (Askin, 2012). **(Primary)**
Indeed, Arroyo and Duque (2004) found one invasive species of grass taking root in Antarctica believed to have been introduced via seeds from tourists, and have warned that seeds from "the Iceland Poppy, Tall Fescue Velvet grass and Annual Winter Grass - all from cold climates and capable of growing in Antarctica" (p. 57) have been found, and their spread may threaten the few native grass species. **(Primary)**
Snyder (2007) further asserted that native Antarctic grass species are particularly vulnerable because they have never had to compete against other species, so they would be easily overrun by the more aggressive invasive strains. **(Primary)**

Paragraph 8:
Many governments already adhere to the established guidelines for scientific cooperation (Australian Antarctic Division, 2011a; Australian Antarctic Division, 2011b; The Secretariat of the Antarctic Treaty, 2011), and this could act as basis for all governments involved in Antarctic tourism to cooperatively monitor their tour companies. **(Primary)**
Restricting this number would ensure that large ships, which require heavily toxic fuels, are not used in the tours (International Maritime Organization, 2011). **(Primary)**

UNIT 3 PART 2

Exercise 1

p. 78

Spanish conquistadors discovered potatoes in Peru in the sixteenth century. They were soon introduced to Europe where they became the staple food in many regions. Some historians believe that the potato, a highly reliable and nutritious crop, eliminated a major source of civil unrest: famine. This led to healthier and increased populations, which in turn resulted in much more stable governments and economies. With this stability, a number of European countries were able to increase their power and eventually project it around the world between 1700 and 1950. In short, the potato was instrumental in helping create the great European empires.

Exercise 2

p. 81

Plagiarized paraphrase
Contemporary society's idea of democracy began in ancient times with the Greeks. However, for the Greeks democracy was a right exercised only by a fraction of the population – landowning men. This elite prohibited men without property and women from voting or having any kind of political involvement. However, this situation was a reflection of society's values and not believed to be a restriction on freedom. To the ancient Greeks, the elite had the responsibility to wield power over all society because they possessed wealth and position, and this gave them an inherited right and responsibility to control the government.

Plagiarized summary
As a reflection of society's values, the ancient Greeks believed that only those of wealth and status were expected to govern.

Exercise 3

p. 82

Acceptable paraphrase
To the ancient Greeks, democracy meant that those possessing high social rank – a minute percentage of society – had the duty to lead the state. Yet, rather than seeing this arrangement as a limitation of freedom, those excluded from political involvement, such as women and men without property, accepted it as an extension of the natural social order. Therefore, though contemporary democracy has evolved from ancient times, in its very early form, only the elite (normally landowning men) governed the entire state.

Acceptable summary
The ancient Greeks believed that only men occupying society's highest class had the right and duty to govern in a democracy.

Exercise 4

p. 82

Best paraphrase: b
a   Meaning different from original – "should change their diet."
c   Meaning different from original – "makes Asians weaker." Excludes information about taste and sodium.

Exercise 5

p. 83

(Example answers)
1. To detect and ultimately abort female fetuses, certain societies use ultrasound devices because of their low cost and portability.
2. A shortage of fresh water to supply the billions in the world is apparently serious enough that it could eventually lead to wars. Among the factors contributing to the drop in fresh water supplies are issues related to the increasing population, sanitation, and the environment.
3. Today's computers can trace their origin back to a person named Alan Turing, who as a student at Cambridge wrote a paper on the algorithm – a central concept to modern computers. Additionally, the concept of artificial intelligence, where computers are capable of thinking, was suggested by him in 1950 and so he is considered by many to be the "Father of Computing."
4. Africa, which in 2011 became second only to Asia in number of cell phone users, is expanding its cellular capabilities to adequately connect the 600 million who have cell phones.
5. Research has shown that having certain blood types increases susceptibility to certain diseases, but no such proof exists showing a relationship between blood types and people's personalities.

Exercise 6

p. 83

Best paraphrase: a
b   only presents one out of the two opinions mentioned in the paragraph.
c   The meaning is different from the original: Donald Asher did not say having a major is unimportant, just that most students pursue careers unrelated to their major.

Exercise 7

p. 84

(Example answers)
1. Hirshi and Gottfredson contend that the propensity to commit crime comes from a person's lack of "self control," whereby the urge to feed one's desires causes one to even break the law.
2. Although used in a variety of genres and originally met with suspicion, the electric guitar grew in importance alongside rock-and-roll and

is now an iconic symbol of rock music and its lifestyle.

3. The majority of American internet users, especially teenagers, use social networking services, which has altered the pace and process of making and maintaining friendships.

Exercise 8

p. 88

(Example answers)

1. In his 1953 speech "No Easy Road to Freedom," Nelson Mandela referred to successful movements around the world to inspire similar change in Africa:

> In China, India, Indonesia and Korea, American, British, Dutch and French Imperialism, based on the concept of the supremacy of Europeans over Asians, has been completely and perfectly exploded. In Malaya and Indo-China British and French imperialisms are being shaken to their foundations by powerful and revolutionary national liberation movements.

2. In *Civilization and Its Discontents*, Freud (1930) asserted that "the liberty of the individual is no gift of civilization. It was greatest before there was any civilization," but admitted, "though then, it is true, it had for the most part no value, since the individual was scarcely in a position to defend it" (p. 42).

UNIT 3 PART 3

Exercise 1

p. 91

Numbered citations:

References

Antarctica annual turnover 900 million U.S. dollars. (2005, March 31). *MercoPress*. Retrieved from http://en.mercopress. com/2005/03/31/antarctica-annual-turnover-900-million-us-dollars ← [6]

Arroyo, C. & Duque, H. (2004). Environmental tragedies in the southern reaches: The human impact on Antarctica. *Nuestra Única Tierra*. 3(1), 46–58. ← [15,18]

Askin, P. (2012, March 6). Alien invasion a threat to Antarctic ecosystem. *Reuters*. Retrieved from http://www.reuters.com/ article/2012/03/06/us-antarctic-seeds-idUSTRE82504V20120306 ← [17]

Associated Press. (2007, November 6). Sunken Antarctic cruise ship left oil spill. *msnbc.com*. Retrieved from http://www.msnbc.msn.com/ id/22039975/ ← [13]

Australian Antarctic Division. (2011a). Australia continues to lead the way in Antarctica. Retrieved from http://www.antarctica.gov. au/media/news/2011/australia-continues-to-lead-the-way-in-antarctica ← [20]

Australian Antarctic Division. (2011b). Training. Retrieved from http://www.antarctica.gov.au/living-http://www.antarctica.gov.au/living-and-working/training ← [20]

Churchill Northern Studies Centre. (2007, March 7). Unique learning vacations. Retrieved from http:// www.churchillscience.ca/index. php?page=vacations ← [5]

Fowler, G. S. (1999). Behavioral and hormonal responses of Magellanic penguins (Spheniscus magellanicus) to tourism and nest site visitation. *Biological Conservation*, *90*(2), 143–149. ← [8]

Grall, J. (1992, September). Antarctic tourism impacts. *TED Case Studies*, *2*(1). Retrieved from http://www1. american.edu/TED/antarct.htm ← [3,10]

Guidelines for Visitors to the Antarctic (2012). International Association of Antarctica Tour Operators (IAATO). Retrieved from http://iaato.org/c/document_ library/get_file?uuid=aed1054d-3e63-4a17-a6cd-a87beb15e287&groupId=10157 ← [11]

International Maritime Organization. (2011, July 29). *Antarctic fuel oil ban and North American ECA MARPOL amendments enter into force on 1 August 2011* [Press Release]. Retrieved from http://www.imo. org/MediaCentre/PressBriefings/ Pages/44-MARPOL-amends.aspx ← [21]

Larson, S. (2012, May 11). More tourists head to Antarctica, affecting the region's ecosystem and science. *Peninsula Press*. Retrieved from http://peninsulapress. com/2012/05/11/more-tourists-head-to-antarctica-affecting-the-regions-ecosystem-and-science/ ← [2,16]

The Secretariat of the Antarctic Treaty. (2011). Environmental protection. Retrieved from http://www.ats.aq/e/ats_environ.htm ← [20]

Shaik, A. (2010, May 4). Antarctic wanderlust. *EJ Magazine*, 2010, Spring. Retrieved from http://news.jrn.msu.edu/ejmagazine/2010/05/04/antarctic-wanderlust-a-booming-tourism-industry-may-harm-earth%E2%80%99s-southernmost-continent/ ← [1, 7 10, 14]

Snyder, J. (2007). Tourism in the polar regions: The sustainability challenge. The United Nations Environment Programme. ← [19]

Tourists in Antarctica cause of major concern. (2009, December 21). *ScienceDaily*. Retrieved from http://www.sciencedaily.com/releases/2009/12/091221130220.htm ← [4]

Trathan, P. N., Forcada, J., Atkinson, R., Downie, R.H., & Shears, J. R. (2008). Population assessments of gentoo penguins (Pygoscelis papua) breeding at an important Antarctic tourist site, Goudier Island, Port Lockroy, Palmer Archipelago, Antarctica. *Biological Conservation*, *141*(12), 3019–3028. ← [9, 12]

Paragraph 2:

1. In fact, from 1990, the number of tourists began to increase to a point where their numbers now exceed the number of scientists (Shaik, 2010).

2. Initially, this was welcomed by research staff whose projects saw a potential funding boost through an increase in visitors, and scientists who stay in Antarctica all year round welcomed the idea of more human contact (Larson, 2012).

3. According to American University, which funds research in the Antarctic, independent tour companies are often unaware of research schedules and bring hundreds of tourists to scientific sites requesting explanations and tours (Grall, 1992).

4. They have had to participate in the rescue of pilots who crashed attempting to break records, or other adventurers who were not prepared for the harsh exposure while trekking in the cold (Tourists in Antarctica, 2009).

Paragraph 3:

5. The funds generated in doing this finance the charity and its research while completely controlling the impact of tourists (Churchill Northern, 2007).

6. Each facility houses and manages the visitors, and the scientists at each station educate and lead tours based on the research focus of each station (Antarctica annual, 2005).

Paragraph 4:

7. The effect that the now nearly 45,000 annual tourists have had on the wildlife in this fragile environment has become a serious concern (Shaik, 2010).

8. Gene S. Fowler (1999), from the University of Washington, documented elevated levels of adrenalin that Magellanic penguins produced upon being excited or scared by a human.

9. According to Trathan, Forcada, Atkinson, Downie, and Shears (2008), the presence of too many humans was the likeliest contributor to a significant drop in gentoo penguin breeding in colonies most exposed to tourists.

Paragraph 5:

10. Tourists often walked dangerously among Weddell seals on the beach, or ventured to within one foot of a penguin's nest for a photo (Grall, 1992; Shaik, 2010),

11. despite the official guidelines of the International Association of Antarctica Tour Operators (IAATO), which advise no closer than 15 feet (Guidelines, 2012).

12. Similarly, reports of other violations include tourists trying to feed penguins, and numerous incidents of tourists chasing seabirds to make them scatter and fly away for a photo (Trathan et al., 2008).

Paragraph 6:

13. The Associated Press (2007) reported one notable example of a cruise ship which sank in Antarctic waters, releasing over 210,000 liters of diesel, 24,000 liters of lubricant, and 1,000 liters of gasoline into the surrounding water, threatening thousands of penguins en route to the continent for mating season.

14. There has been at least one other report of a ship sinking, and several reports of ships coming too close to shore and running aground (Shaik, 2010).

15. Marcus Zylkstra, an environmentalist in Antarctica, has criticized the condition of a number of American stations as having "decades' worth of human excrement, sewage, gas and oil leaking from broken-down and abandoned vehicles, and numerous piles of discarded garbage and debris" (as cited in Arroyo & Duque, 2004, p. 52).

Paragraph 7:

16. Larson (2012) reports that microbes from foreign environments cling to the boots and jackets of disembarking visitors and infect the flora and fauna in potentially unpredictable ways.

17. Studies have confirmed that virtually every visitor coming to the region carries a plethora of microscopic life forms alien to Antarctica. In addition, tourists unknowingly transport tiny seeds which are carried in their clothing (Askin, 2012).

18. Indeed, Arroyo and Duque (2004) found one invasive species of grass taking root in Antarctica believed to have been introduced via seeds from tourists, and have warned that seeds from "the Iceland Poppy, Tall Fescue Velvet grass and Annual Winter Grass – all from cold climates and capable of growing in Antarctica" (p. 57) have been found, and their spread may threaten the few native grass species.

19. Snyder (2007) further asserted that native Antarctic grass species are particularly vulnerable because they have never had to compete against other species, so they would be easily overrun by the more aggressive invasive strains.

Paragraph 8:

20. Many governments already adhere to the established guidelines for scientific cooperation (Australian Antarctic Division, 2011a; Australian Antarctic Division, 2011b; The Secretariat of the Antarctic Treaty, 2011), and this could act as a basis for all governments involved in Antarctic tourism to cooperatively monitor their tour companies.

21. Restricting this number would ensure that large ships, which require heavily toxic fuels, are not used in the tours (International Maritime Organization, 2011).

1. Citations 10, 20 – citations separated by a semi-colon.

2. Citation 12 – citation of the same people made earlier (9); "et al." indicates there are other authors of the source information.

3. Citation 15 – name mentioned in the sentence is the originator of the information found in Arroyo & Duque.

4. Citation 15 – use "&" for citation inside parentheses.

5. Citations 15, 18 – the source is particularly long; the page number helps pinpoint exactly where the information is.

6. Citation 20 – Australian Antarctic Division is the same source of two entries with the same year on the References list; "a" and "b" distinguishes the two entries.

Exercise 2

p. 92

1. No.

2. Yes – specific data which likely came from a primary source.

3. No.

4. Yes – information this specific often comes from one primary source.

5. Yes – the part about Singapore's fertility rate is specific; however, the 2.1 figure by itself does not need to be cited.

6. No.

7. No – has become common knowledge; impossible to cite every biologist who believes this.

8. No.

9. Yes – highly subjective viewpoint on Confucianism.

10. Yes – possible to cite the more prominent NGOs that believe this.

UNIT 3 PART 4

Exercise 1

p. 95

(Example answers)
1. believe / argue / contend that
2. have demonstrated / shown / proven
3. indicates / implies / suggests that

Exercise 2

p. 96

(Example answers)
1. stress / emphasize
2. applauded / praised / recognized
3. criticized / singled out / condemned

Exercise 3

p. 96

(Example answers)
1. characterize / describe
2. described / viewed / referred to
3. interpret / view / describe

Exercise 4

p. 99

1. c
2. a
3. c
4. a
5. a
6. c
7. a
8. a
9. b
10. b

UNIT 4 PART 1

Exercise 1

p. 105

The globalization of industrial agriculture has also failed to provide the promised economic benefits to Central American farmers. In order to compete in global trade, <u>many</u> farmers have turned to monoculture, growing <u>only</u> one crop rather than multiple crops, to maximize yields. Statistics from the World Currency Group (2008) <u>suggest</u> that this change in agricultural practice has <u>likely</u> contributed to a reduction in rural unemployment throughout Central America by <u>about</u> 4% since 2001. Although the change to specialized, high-demand export crops <u>may</u> account for this decrease, employment figures <u>alone</u> cannot <u>definitively</u> show that the situation has improved. <u>In fact</u>, other economic indicators <u>appear</u> to negate the importance of the employment numbers. Recent figures from the Central American Agribusiness Association (2011) <u>clearly</u> indicate that real income levels during the same time period also decreased. It <u>may be possible</u> to conclude, therefore, that while monoculture <u>can</u> increase the demand for labor, its higher yields <u>tend</u> to reduce the global market value of the crop, lower profits for farmers, and maintain poverty in the region.

Exercise 2

p. 105

(Example answers)
1. Research indicates that children are somewhat better second language learners than adults.

2. Analysts seem to agree that the United Nations has successfully intervened in regional armed conflicts in some areas of the world.

3. Most teenagers consider social networking sites an important part of their friendship experiences.

4. It may be that the international appeal of the Hollywood film industry is due to its financial and technical power.

5. Scientists suggest that global warming will be one of the most catastrophic events in human history.

Exercise 3

p. 106

(Example answers)
1. The fashion industry is indeed one area in which it is crucial that models have good looks.

2. In some cases, animal rights organizations demand that animals never be used in experiments.

3. Medical evidence clearly shows that regular cardiovascular exercise will certainly reduce the chance of heart disease.

4. A strong familiarity with computer technology is undoubtedly useful for most administrative office jobs.

5. After earthquakes, trained sniffer dogs play a significant role in finding survivors buried under collapsed buildings.

Exercise 4

p. 107

(Example answers)
1. Kovacs (2012) asserts that developing countries would greatly benefit from removing restrictions on trade.

2. Globalization undoubtedly leads to the "Englishization" of the world as people increasingly need to speak English to participate in the global economy.

3. Corruption is a serious problem in developing countries, but Sanchez (2010) contends it is also a significant problem in developed countries.

4. Most new medicines are widely available in developed countries, but they are rarely available in many developing parts of the world

5. Environmental degradation in the developing world is likely not caused by the indigenous people, but more likely by multinational companies in industrial countries taking their natural resources.

UNIT 4 PART 2

Exercise 1

p. 113

(Example answers)
1. Historians argue over what the actual Native American population was before European colonization: as low as 30 million for some, as high as 60 million for others.
   Historians argue over what the actual Native American population was before European colonization; some estimate as low as 30 million, while others as high as 60 million.

2. Sony's market value is $21 billion; Samsung's value is $162 billion.
   Although Sony is valued at $21 billion, Samsung is almost eight times larger at $162 billion.

3. Both the words "snake" and "sneak" originate from the same proto Indo-European word "snag," which means to crawl or creep.
   The proto Indo-European word "snag," which means to crawl or creep, is the origin of two common and similar English words: "snake" and "sneak."

4. Despite being considered the best in the world and noted for its intense flavor, full body, and mild aroma, Kenya coffee is still mostly produced on small-scale farms.

   Kenya coffee is considered the best in the world, as it is noted for its intense flavor, full body, and mild aroma. However, about 70 percent of it is still produced on small-scale farms.

5. 2010 statistics show a rapid increase in online newspaper readership; there are 1.9 billion online readers worldwide.

   According to 2010 statistics, online newspaper readership has increased significantly. Hence, there are 1.9 billion readers worldwide.

Exercise 2

p. 116

(Example answers)

1. Likewise, they argue over how much of the population was killed by European diseases, with some claiming 40% and others claiming 80%.

2. To further illustrate this difference, according to *Forbes* (2011), Samsung is the 26th largest company in the world; Sony the 477th.

3. Similarly, the word "snail" has the same origin.

4. Also grown on small-scale farms is Kenyan tea, which is similarly noted for its full body and malty flavor.

5. Despite this, there are still more traditional readers of newspapers: 2.3 billion, which is a slight increase from before.

Exercise 3

p. 119

1. a (It is not necessary to state the agent of the action because it is clear that "theater companies" "perform" *Hamlet*.)

2. b (The first sentence describes the report's impact – an action or effect. Therefore, "caused confusion" better stresses the effect.)

3. b (The first sentence emphasizes people – "the average citizen." The active sentence "people have" better continues the focus on humans.)

4. b (The first sentence refers to a survey about dissatisfaction, emphasizing actions rather than people. "Waiting times" keeps the focus on the abstract process.)

5. a (The first sentence talks about "local people," so people are the focus of the text, rather than actions. The active sentence "they were afraid" emphasizes these people rather than abstracting the process with a nominalization "fear of crime.")

6. a (The first sentence talks about players. The passive "they may be" keeps the emphasis on the players, who are more important than the rival fans.)

Exercise 4

p. 120

(Example answers)

1. Active voice: Nuclear watchdog groups investigate the safety of nuclear power plants.

   Passive voice: The safety of nuclear power plants is investigated by nuclear watchdog groups.

   Nominalization: The investigation of nuclear power plant safety is done by nuclear watchdog groups.

2. Active voice: Political parties surveyed citizens' opinions regarding the proposal to increase consumption tax.

   Passive voice: Citizens' opinions regarding the proposal to increase consumption tax were surveyed by political parties.

   Nominalization: The surveying of citizens' opinions regarding the proposal to increase consumption tax was done by political parties.

3. Active voice: The Ministry of Education is examining how high-speed internet can deliver education more efficiently and effectively.

   Passive voice: How high-speed internet can deliver education more efficiently and effectively is being examined by the Ministry of Education.

   Nominalization: An examination of how high-speed internet can deliver education more efficiently and effectively is being done by the Ministry of Education.

4. Active voice: International human rights organizations protest the unequal treatment of women in advanced and developing countries all over the world.

   Passive voice: The unequal treatment of women in advanced and developing countries all over the world is protested by international human rights organizations.

   Nominalization: The protest of the unequal treatment of women in advanced and developing countries all over the world is done by international human rights organizations.

5. Active voice: Economists have hypothesized a correlation between the world economic downturn of 2008 and banks being connected by globalization.

   Passive voice: A correlation between the world economic downturn of 2008 and banks being connected by globalization has been hypothesized by economists.

   Nominalization: Hypothesizing the correlation between the world economic downturn of 2008 and banks being connected by globalization has been done by economists.

UNIT 4 PART 3

p. 127

NOTE: Below is a paragraph-by-paragraph comparison of the error-filled essay from the textbook (above) and an edited version (below). Please see where edits were made and use this to help form questions to guide students when editing the textbook's essay (e.g., *There are two mistakes in the first sentence. What are they?*).

(Example answer)

Essay and References list from textbook:

Social Networking

Many people have used the internet, especially tenagers. Tenager across the Globe are learning how to become internet superstars. In an era of increasing digital connection, social networking sites (SNS) are gaining in popularity and changing the way that generations of internet users communicate with friend and person that they have never met before. More people are using SNS to keep up with people they know and meeting new people. Older genrations claims that SNS interaction is a cheapened or superficial forms of communication and may slow or harm teenagers' ability to grow into young adults who are able to be sociable in society. However, they are wrong because SNS allows them to do many things. For example, mold their identities, broadcast their ideas, and connect with friends both old and new. Some of my friends have even met their spouse through SNS. SNS are excellent because they offer a variety of ways are rewriting the way that teenagers grow as human beings.

SNS allows teenager to mold their identities. Cool sites such as Facbook, which is currently the biggest and best of the SNS, allows users to add a variety of information about themselves to their profiles which can be seen by many people. While all users opt to display basic details such as their gander, birthday and relationship status in their profiles, they also include items such as their favorite books, movies and music (Catherine Dwyer) which help shape their identity even more. Tiffany mentioned, teenagers also feel comfortable displaying their sexual orientation, religion, and political affiliations, and this shows that teenagers are using the SNS experience to help control their overall identity (Tiffany Pempek). Teenagers shape their identity this way and they spend a lot of time on it. This large amount of time teenagers spend shows that they value the attention they get from people who look at their profile. This means they find value face-to-face contact less. It is clear that teenagers spend a lot of time constructing their profile on the internet in SNS. This is a new and better way for teenagers to mold an identity which many people can see.

SNS are changing the way people interact with other people by providing a new form of communication among people. Teenagers are now easily able to broadcast their ideas via one-to-many broadcasting. For instance, it is possible to post messages on a friend's wall through Facebook or share an witty remark with one's followers on Twitter, and these remarks are freely available for other people to see. Twitter is actually more popular than Facebook. SNS are able to have video and photos uploaded. An advantage for teenagers.

Social networking sites gives people who has online access a way to maintain friendships. A person joins a particular SNS because he was invited by a friend. They can stay in touch with friends more easily. Especially with people who live in a foreign country. People can use SNS to find new friends who may share similar interests. The Twiter network is growing rapidly and always recommends following other users who comment on similar topics (Mashable), so any person who has an account with Twiter can quickly establish connections with individuals who may share similar interests virtually. Facbook allows users to help their contacts find friends on top of the onese they already have through a system which recommends other possible friends. I like how SNS inform me of people I know and which someone else I know knows, and so I can friend these people. It's easy and anyone can realize how SNS can improve their lives by becoming friends with everyone.

In conclusion, through the use of social networking sites, which are constantly developing, tenager are maturing in society faster and quicker than their parents, who are not able to experience the advantages of SNS. Such as establishing their identity or making new friends. Teenagers become smarter because they can exchange opinions with everyone, and having many friends makes teenagers more popular. Research also show that people who do not use SNS have a big disadvantage when trying to find a job. Social networking sites will continue in the future, so it is necessary for teenagers to learn how to interact socially online if they want to be popular and find a job in the fture.

References

Adam Ostrow. "Twitter Starts Offering Personalized Suggestions of Users to Follow." Mashable .com. <http://mashable.com/2010/07/30/twitter-suggestions-for-you/>.

Catherine Dwyer, Starr Roxanne Hiltz and Katia Passerini. "Trust and privacy concern within social networking sites: A comparison of Facebook and MySpace." 2007.

Jilin Chen, et al. 'Make New Friends, but Keep the Old' – Recommending People on Social Networking Sites." <http://portal.acm.org/citation.cfm?id=1518701&picked=prox&cfid=3010584&cftoken=38427102>.

Tiffany A. Pempek, Yevdokiya A. Yermolayeva, and Sandra L. Calvert. Journal of Applied Developmental Psychology <http://www.sciencedirect.com/science/>.

Edited essay and References list:

Social Networking Sites Redefine Social Growth

Teenagers across the globe are learning how to become internet superstars. In an era of increasing digital connection, social networking sites (SNS) are gaining in popularity and changing the way that generations of internet users communicate with friends and people that they have never met before. In addition to privacy concerns, older generations have claimed that SNS interaction is a cheapened or superficial form of communication and may slow or harm teenagers' ability to grow into socially competent young adults. However, SNS are rewriting the way that younger generations grow as human beings because they allow them to mold their identities, broadcast their ideas, and connect with friends both old and new.

One way that SNS have redefined the experience of growing up is by providing young people with more control over the construction of their public identities. Sites such as Facebook, which is currently one of the largest online communities in the world, allow users to add a variety of personalized information to their public profiles. While the majority of users opt to display basic details such as their gender, birthday, and relationship status in their profiles, a large number also choose to include more identity-categorizing items such as their favorite books, movies, and music (Dwyer et al., p. 7). Impressively, many others feel comfortable displaying their sexual orientation, religion, and political affiliations as well, and this is a clear indication that youths are using the SNS experience to help control their overall identity (Pempek et al., p. 233). Such tailoring of one's virtual image is something that many teens spend a considerable amount of time on. Indeed, the social value of one's online presence is easy to understand when considering how often content from SNS is discussed offline among peers. It is therefore clear that online profile construction is a new way that younger generations understand and mold their public identity.

In addition to identity construction, SNS are changing interaction patterns by providing a new public form of communication. People are now easily able to broadcast their ideas via one-to-many broadcasting. For instance, it is possible to post messages on a friend's wall through Facebook or share a witty remark with one's followers on Twitter, and these remarks are freely available for other people to see and react to. According to recent research, this public style of communication is preferred two-to-one over the private messaging abilities that are built into Facebook and Twitter (Pempek et al., p. 235). Combined with the video and photo uploading capabilities of many SNS, this broadcasting has the potential to give users constant feedback on the way that they present both themselves and their thoughts. In short, today's youth have the option to be continually connected to, and interact with, their community of friends even if they are not able to converse in person.

Finally, social networking sites give digitally connected teenagers and young adults an integral way to maintain friendships. Many people join a particular SNS because they were invited by an offline friend. They appreciate the ability to be able to stay in touch with friends who live in different regions, and this can be especially helpful for high school friends who attend different universities. Moreover, people can also use SNS to find new friends who may share similar interests. The rapidly growing Twitter network routinely recommends following other users who comment on similar topics (Ostrow), so any person with an account can quickly establish virtual connections with like-minded individuals. Facebook offers similar suggestions and also allows users to help their contacts find additional friends through a recommendations system. Furthermore, most SNS inform users of their mutual connections with a third party, and this can also assist in encouraging people to "friend" someone that they have never met offline (Chen et al., p. 206). As a result, it is not uncommon for internet-enabled teenagers to be in friendly contact with literally dozens more people than was true for their counterparts just a decade ago.

In conclusion, through the use of ever-developing social networking sites, recent and future generations of teenagers are navigating a very different social maturation process compared to what their parents experienced. Critically, young people are finding new ways to establish their identity through careful molding of their SNS profiles. Accordingly, they learn the best ways to offer their opinions and ideas for public consumption by communicating in a one-to-many fashion online. In addition, thanks to the built-in friend recommendation features of many SNS, young people can both establish and maintain friendships in a digital environment. Even though the popular social networking sites of today may fall out of favor in the future, learning to interact socially online is clearly becoming a necessary part of growing up. Current trends indicate that young people will rely heavily on SNS as a preferred form of communication for the foreseeable future.

References

Chen, J., Geyer, W., Dugan, C., Muller, M., & Guy, I. (2009, April 6). "Make new friends, but keep the old" – Recommending people on social networking sites. *CHI 2009 – Online Relationships (2009)*. 201–210. ACM Digital Library. Retrieved from http://portal.acm.org/citation.cfm?id=1518701&picked=prox&cfid=3010584&cftoken=38427102

Dwyer, C., Hiltz, S. R., & Passerini, K. (2007). Trust and privacy concern within social networking sites: A comparison of Facebook and MySpace. *AMCIS 2007 Proceedings*. Paper 339. Retrieved from http://aisel.aisnet.org/amcis2007/339

Ostrow, A. (2010, July 30). Twitter starts offering personalized suggestions of users to follow. *Mashable.com*. Retrieved from http://mashable.com/2010/07/30/twitter-suggestions-for-you/

Pempek, T. A., Yermolayeva, Y. A., & Calvert, S. L. (2009, May–June). College students' social networking on Facebook. *Journal of Applied Developmental Psychology 30*(3), 227–238. Retrieved from http://www.sciencedirect.com/science/

Appendix C

Review activity

p. 137

(Example answers)

1. One major impact Europeans had on Native Americans was the introduction of horses. Horses were first brought to North America in the sixteenth century and rapidly transformed the lives of Native Americans. Morrison (2009) notes that explorers from France who came during the 1700s were astonished by how integral horses had become to the lives of Native Americans. The impact on the lives of Indian tribes in the plains was particularly strong, as their ability to move quickly over wide areas of land allowed them to expand their territory, improved their hunting skills, and made them better fighters in battle.

2. The ancient and modern Olympics share similarities in terms of athletes' attitudes towards winning. As is the case today, a victory in the ancient Olympics greatly boosted social status. Because of the strong incentive winning presented, many athletes chose to consume drugs in order to gain a competitive advantage. When writing about the Olympics over 2,000 years ago, Filostratos mentioned the use of performance-enhancing substances in *Gymnasticos*: "Such is their desire for glory and riches, Olympic Games athletes eat bread containing potentially dangerous juice of the plant poppy opium, or potions made from a plant called hippouris for muscle mass and increased strength" (as cited in Stamkos, 2004, p. 75). Although the substances used may have changed, the recent spate of scandals involving performance-enhancing drugs has revealed that athletes' appetites for victory, even at the expense of fairness, have changed little since the games began.

3. The modern wireless society can allow working mothers to stay at home with their children and maintain their careers. Previously, mothers often had to sacrifice an important part of their lives through choosing to stay at home with their children, and abandon their careers, because doing both effectively was extremely difficult. However, recent research has found that when using wireless devices to access their jobs, mothers working from home reported a greater level of happiness in being able to provide for their children and an increase in productivity when they were working (Jomada, Ng, & Reger, 2012; Elliott et al., 2013). The wireless society, therefore, cannot only provide women more control over their lives, but create a desirable balance between life and work.

4. The development of India's economy has disrupted the traditional system of social stratification and replaced it with one based on achievement and income. As opportunities for wealth and status have greatly increased, young people, eager to move upwards, have shifted their focus away from traditional ideas about caste and instead place importance on skills and experience when forming business associations. Indeed, Chatterjee (2009) reports that for influential businesspeople under age 40, 84% claim that the decision to employ workers or form partnerships is based on motivation, ability, past successes, and intelligence, rather than caste. With increasingly less emphasis being placed on birth privilege, people who in the past would have likely found themselves doomed to a lifetime of poverty are reaching the top of the social ladder.

5. Coral reefs must be safeguarded against further harm, as they are a crucial part of both their ecosystems and the lives of people living around them. First of all, further loss of coral reefs would have a catastrophic impact on marine life. Pauline Santos of the Pacific Conservation Institute notes: "Coral reefs are the rainforest of the sea. Over 25% of fish in the ocean and as many as two million marine species live in or depend on coral reefs for survival" (as cited in Foster, 2012, p. 93). As even small changes in an ecosystem can have wide-ranging impacts, such a large disruption would likely do irreversible damage throughout the world's oceans. A loss in coral reefs would also have devastating consequences for people, particularly in towns and villages in developing countries dependent on coral reefs. In addition to protecting the coastline, the reefs are an important source of medicine, tourism, and food, vital for the economic well-being of numerous small communities in developing nations; their disappearance would amount to a loss of roughly $30 to $40 billion per year (Obingwe, 2010). Clearly, the loss of coral reefs would also incur a significant economic loss worldwide to many industries, but especially affect poorer countries which could have entire communities devastated by the loss of their main economic resource.